D1403631

Praise for *Playbook for Success*

"Nancy has clearly experienced so much success in the world of basketball. She also possesses many great leadership qualities that have driven her to success off the court. She is a committed, confident, and resourceful person who has demonstrated the ability to lead people and accomplish great things. She is a true Hall of Famer not only in basketball, but also in life."

—NORBY WILLIAMSON
EXECUTIVE SENIOR VICE PRESIDENT OF STUDIO AND
EVENT PRODUCTION ESPN

"Nancy has done something essential with *Playbook for Success*. She has produced a roadmap for decision making. She demonstrates that leadership requires ability to persuade and to make those who follow stronger as they move forward. Her passion to perform in sports and business is captured on every page. She has hit the most important shot of her illustrious career with this book!"

—JERRY JONES
OWNER OF THE DALLAS COWBOYS

"There is no doubt that Nancy Lieberman's personal playbook for life has been one geared to success. I have known her for most of our lives, and through all of her endeavors, she has demonstrated that hard work and a strategic approach to solving problems is what will get you far. We can all learn from her playbook."

—DONNA ORENDER
WNBA PRESIDENT

"I've been exposed to countless 'how to succeed' books over the years, but Nancy Lieberman's *Playbook for Success* is my favorite. It contains the perfect blend of humor, personal experiences, strategies, and stories that make this book a highly entertaining read. It provides a legitimate pathway to a life of significance. It's a truly amazing work!"

—SAM CASTER
CEO MANNATECH

"It has been our pleasure to know Nancy on a personal level, and gradually come to learn how very many layers make up this phenomenal human being. While sharing her sense of humor, drive, success, and support of others Nancy has managed to write a concise, thoughtful, and applicable plan for success in business and personal goals. Nancy has been able to bridge the gap between team sports and success in business. Her book is not only a must read, but a must give."

—MELISSA AND RUSSELL B. WIGHT
DIRECTOR OF ALEXANDER, INC.

"Nancy Lieberman is the best there ever was. An American legend, she brought home the gold for the U.S.A. She inspires millions of girls and boys to reach for the stars, to do their best, and to never give up. Business is a lot like basketball, and Nancy tells us—in words we can all understand—how to build great company teams and win competitive games in the economic market place."

—SAM WYLY
BUSINESS ENTREPRENEUR/
AUTHOR OF *1,000 DOLLARS & AN IDEA*

"At first glance one might think a *Playbook for Success* is a book written for women. However, a *Playbook for Success* is a 'must read' for every teenage boy and girl, young man and women, and business executive who is passionate about being a better person, student, player, leader, and business executive."

—JERRY COLANGELO
FORMER MLB, NBA, WNBA, NHL OWNER
NATIONAL DIRECTOR OF USA BASKETBALL

"Nancy's *Playbook for Success* has rationalized clearly for me the relationship between a sports career or effort and overall success as an individual or team member. Trying harder, as she constantly brings up, is also the key factor in any success story. As an athlete I have been limited by pursuing a business career at the same time, but I am enjoying both enormously."

—JORGE PAULO LEMANN
BUSINESS ENTREPRENEUR

"In sports and in business, teamwork is essential. When you have the right people in the right places working together to do the right thing, miracles happen. Nancy's book teaches us a lot about the importance of teamwork and business."

—ROGER STAUBACH
HALL OF FAME QUARTERBACK

PLAYBOOK
FOR
SUCCESS

PLAYBOOK
FOR
SUCCESS

A Hall of Famer's Business Tactics for Teamwork and Leadership

NANCY LIEBERMAN

WILEY

John Wiley & Sons, Inc.

Copyright © 2010 by Nancy Lieberman. All rights reserved.

Published by John Wiley & Sons, Inc., Hoboken, New Jersey.
Published simultaneously in Canada.

No part of this publication may be reproduced, stored in a retrieval system, or transmitted in any form or by any means, electronic, mechanical, photocopying, recording, scanning, or otherwise, except as permitted under Section 107 or 108 of the 1976 United States Copyright Act, without either the prior written permission of the Publisher, or authorization through payment of the appropriate per-copy fee to the Copyright Clearance Center, Inc., 222 Rosewood Drive, Danvers, MA 01923, (978) 750-8400, fax (978) 646-8600, or on the web at www.copyright.com. Requests to the Publisher for permission should be addressed to the Permissions Department, John Wiley & Sons, Inc., 111 River Street, Hoboken, NJ 07030, (201) 748-6011, fax (201) 748-6008, or online at http://www.wiley.com/go/permissions.

Limit of Liability/Disclaimer of Warranty: While the publisher and author have used their best efforts in preparing this book, they make no representations or warranties with respect to the accuracy or completeness of the contents of this book and specifically disclaim any implied warranties of merchantability or fitness for a particular purpose. No warranty may be created or extended by sales representatives or written sales materials. The advice and strategies contained herein may not be suitable for your situation. You should consult with a professional where appropriate. Neither the publisher nor author shall be liable for any loss of profit or any other commercial damages, including but not limited to special, incidental, consequential, or other damages.

For general information on our other products and services or for technical support, please contact our Customer Care Department within the United States at (800) 762-2974, outside the United States at (317) 572-3993 or fax (317) 572-4002.

Wiley also publishes its books in a variety of electronic formats. Some content that appears in print may not be available in electronic books. For more information about Wiley products, visit our web site at www.wiley.com.

ISBN 978-0-470-63552-0 (cloth)
ISBN 978-0-470-90504-3 (ebk)
ISBN 978-0-470-90506-7 (ebk)
ISBN 978-0-470-90507-4 (ebk)

Printed in the United States of America

10 9 8 7 6 5 4 3 2 1

For every person that wants more from themselves and in life—trust your heart and love what you do. Just don't talk about it, be about it. Mom and TJ, you are the stars of my dream journey and with your love, I am who I said I would be.

Nancy

CONTENTS

FOREWORD

My friendship with Nancy goes back almost 30 years. Our basketball careers have been intertwined as we watched and cheered for each other's success. As point guards, our competitiveness, leadership, and overall commitment to make the people around us better helped lead us to our true calling as entrepreneurs.

With this book, Lady Magic delivers again! It fills your appetite with wisdom, insight, and motivation. She's a Hall of Famer and a winner. You can use her *Playbook for Success* as your daily routine for business and life's success. She has taught countless men and women to have the mind-set of a champion and to never fear success.

I had Larry Bird to help push me to greatness by winning five NBA Titles with the Los Angeles Lakers, but Nancy overcame the obstacles of not having a rival or WNBA in her prime but still had the passion and purpose to come back and be the oldest player in the inaugural season of the WNBA.

I didn't know it at the time, but Nancy tells the story of us sitting at the 1996 Olympics in Atlanta. I asked her while we were watching a game, "So are you going to play in the WNBA next year?" She said, "I hope so." I said, "Nancy then you better get home and start training." She did, and thus made history at the age of 39 with the Phoenix Mercury. Today my friend is still making history. She is a successful business leader, inspiring role model, and the first female to ever coach in the NBA's Development League team for the Dallas Mavericks. She definitely has a roadmap for success on and off the court. Her book *Playbook for Success* is nothing more than how she has led her life. Well done my friend!

—Earvin "Magic" Johnson

Acknowledgments

Often in life, we get pigeonholed by others, people who *think* they know who we really are. I am a basketball player, so what can I possibly have to tell people, especially women, about business? My answer is, I have a lot of life to share.

I also have a lot of thanks to share with those who helped me in the writing of this book.

To Dan Ambrosio at John Wiley & Sons, Inc.: You are priceless for giving me a platform from which I can share my experiences. Special thanks to Ashley Allison and Peter Knox.

To Jared Sharp at PTA: I am deeply grateful.

To Christine Moore: For all your painstaking time spent editing my manuscript and working through my tender-loving sarcasm and humor.

To Sally Giddens Stephenson: You worked the "two-minute drill" like nobody else in dealing with our deadline. I am so thankful for your willingness to pursue this project and for your focus to succeed. You are a true winner!

To Nena Madonia: I was told a few years ago that Jan Miller was the Michael Jordan of publishing agents, and she has the rings to prove it. Michael had Scottie Pippen, and Jan has Nena Madonia, who was my "go-to player" on this book. I have never seen you have a bad day, and your spirit and love never wavered for my vision for *Playbook for Success*. I'm deeply grateful.

To be successful, I have always needed someone who had my back. This responsibility falls daily on the shoulders of my favorite MSU Spartan, Theresa Pusateri. She is more than my trusted assistant; she is a true rock of a human being. She keeps my days organized. She is my memory, my right and my left hands. T, you have been a true blessing to me and TJ Thank you for your endless hours to help keep me focused, allowing me to make a difference for others!

TJ, I wake up each day proud to be your mom, and wanting to be your hero in life. I love you dearly. And to many of my friends and family who heard me say, "I'll get back to you; I have to finish my book," thank you all for your patience.

1

Why Sports and Business for Women?

Never stop working, wanting, or dreaming.

—Nancy Lieberman

How does a poor girl from Far Rockaway, New York, defy the odds and become a Hall of Fame basketball player, coach, author, television analyst, entrepreneur, and mom? The simple answer is luck, and in many cases, I created my own luck. However, the complete story about how I got from there to here involves love, passion, faith, vision, fearlessness, and a stubborn will to succeed.

I've lived my own *Playbook for Success*, and it comes naturally to me. Now I'm putting it all down in this book to share what I've learned with you: the secrets and steps that will take you to new levels of success you didn't think were possible. Well, they are! I know this from firsthand experience. My life has been about overachieving and showing people that they, too, could do anything they wanted to do—*if* they had a plan and were willing to put in the hard work.

The streets of New York gave me a toughness that has helped me to survive and keep moving forward when everything seemed hopeless. If not for the playbook provided to me at a young age by Lavoiser Lamar, one of my coaches in Harlem, you might not be reading my book—or absorbing and utilizing this plan for your own personal growth and success.

My days on the courts proved invaluable in developing my competitive spirit. They taught me not only how to win but also how to use my losses as tools for evaluating myself, zeroing in on my weaknesses, and turning them into strengths. I had to be honest: Did I make myself and others around me better? Now, you might be shaking your head and wondering, "How does athletic experience translate into business success?" Well, whether you're a female doctor, lawyer, stockbroker, sales or marketing associate, business

3

manager or owner, it's still a man's world, and we women must be able to communicate, interact, earn respect, lead, and impact everyone who comes in contact with us. *Playbook for Success: A Hall of Famer's Business Tactics for Teamwork and Leadership* will let you in on something men have been doing for a very long time: connecting through, and using what they've learned by participating in, sports, to get ahead in the business world.

I made history as the youngest Olympic basketball player ever, but that wouldn't have happened if I hadn't played in the schoolyard against the boys. They pushed me, made me work harder, and taught me to show up—and toughen up, both mentally and physically—if I intended to play in their game. Man, did I take some bruises to my body and ego early on! But those lessons taught me to keep coming back and get better. Along the way, I developed a successful strategy for self-improvement—one that I still utilize today.

Want to know how I always got into the basketball games at Harlem's Rucker Park? Simple: To be allowed to play, you had to hit your foul shots. The first 10 players to do so were automatically in the game. Well, I couldn't dunk, and I wasn't as fast or as strong as the guys, but I could hit my foul shots. When the baddest dudes with all the talent couldn't, I *could*. That, my friend, is what got me on the court time after time, and left those guys who threw up the bricks from the foul line sitting in the stands waiting for their turn to play. I found my strength and a strategy, and I used them to be successful. I didn't know at the time that I was using a *Playbook for Success*, but I was.

Once I proved myself to be a worthy contributor, the guys began to respect me, protect me, and share with me what they knew about the game. To this day, so many of those simple but vital strategies I learned back then play a huge part in my interactions as a business leader—with both men and women. I'm in the business of sports, a multibillion-dollar industry; in fact, it's the fourteenth largest-grossing industry sector—larger than the steel and railroad industries. My point is, love and/or knowledge of sports can bring you into the loop and help you to generate trust, close a deal, and build lasting friendships. Sports can teach us girls that we can do anything. Vice President Joe Biden made that point in an interview on ESPN, given when he attended the 2010 women's basketball championship game between Connecticut and Stanford. He sat a couple of rows from the floor, at center court, with his two young granddaughters. When asked why he was there, Biden replied: "I tell my daughter and my granddaughters they can do anything a boy can do. Sports gives you overwhelming confidence."

Sure, I played the game, but even those who didn't can use the same strategies and techniques I developed as an athlete to conduct business on an equal playing field with both men and women. How did my involvement with sports contribute to my successful business development? Let me count the ways:

1. Leadership skills
2. Discipline
3. Ability to participate on a team
4. Communication
5. Self-confidence
6. Goal-setting skills
7. Vision
8. Positive attitude
9. Perseverance
10. Resilience
11. Healthy competiveness

Wow, that's a long list. And let me add that you find your love and passion in sports; they teach you how to read people and stand shoulder-to-shoulder with them in the trenches.

Why do I use a playbook analogy? Because, throughout my life I have lived the connection between sports and business. Women who never played sports or who aren't interested in them often find themselves relegated to the sidelines and lacking vital knowledge. That's why I believe strongly that all businesswomen need my

Playbook for Success. So many of us were given the chance to participate in sports in our youth—and it was the purest form of competition. We played with and against one another in the neighborhood. We watched sports together on television. I remember to this day getting chills when the New York Knicks won the NBA title in 1970 against the Los Angeles Lakers. I can recall injured team captain Willis Reed limping out of the tunnel for his dramatic entrance for game 7 of that series. Similarly, I can still see Michael Jordan hitting a buzzer-beater to win a game.

Sports stir emotions that connect strangers to each other. Just think what that same experience can do for you in a meeting, with a key client, or among your staff. It reinforces success for both men and women; it's an economic force. It can help you communicate, relate to clients, and grow your sales.

Consider a survey conducted by Oppenheimer Funds a few years ago that surveyed 401 female senior executives. The results found that 82 percent of them had played organized sports after elementary school. Coincidence? I don't think so. When asked, the respondents claimed that their experiences playing team sports contributed significantly to their business success and provided them with leadership skills, greater discipline, and the ability to function well as part of a team. They also said sports helped them deal more effectively with failure and gave them a competitive edge.

No doubt about it: The workplace favors athletes, whether male *or* female. A sports background enhances your passion for winning and teaches you "soft skills," such as how to read nonverbal clues, focus in the midst of chaos, and support others. I know this because I have more than 35 years experience playing and coaching basketball, starting and running several successful businesses, and working within ESPN and other major companies. Thanks to these experiences, I have developed a passion for winning and working at a higher level. In this book I want to teach *you* the "plays" you need to master to reach that same level of success—no matter how big or small the league you're playing in.

Being able to communicate and bond in the workplace is absolutely critical, and I assure you that two of your greatest assets will be developing an appreciation for sports and understanding their connection to business. Yes, sports! Reading the red (i.e., sports) section of *USA Today*, for example, is a great way to bond and develop friendships before any deal is ever discussed. Think about it: Don't you enjoy working with people you like and connect with? More important, if you can hang with the boys, you can sell to the boys!

When I emphasize how important sports are to your career, I don't just mean being able to participate in the discussion about the big playoff game the night before (though that always helps); I am talking about competition in a larger sense—being able to apply to the workplace the valuable lessons of teamwork and leadership we can learn in sports. I firmly believe that success flows from becoming the best you can be, from constant self-improvement, and from the pursuit of personal excellence. This is the philosophy that underlies every play in this book. Once you tap into the ability to recognize your own potential, the rest of the plays will follow.

The workplace is as competitive as any playing field, and knowing how to compete is a big part of learning how to win consistently, and can give you an immediate advantage over a colleague who never set foot on a soccer field, wielded a lacrosse stick, or dribbled a basketball.

But what if that nonathletic colleague is you? Never fear! That's what *Playbook for Success* is designed to do: arm you with the sports-themed tools of a professional athlete, no matter what your sports background. You don't have to be a player to understand and use sports to get ahead in business. You can be a fan—anyone can. Whether it's your hometown team, or the team in the city in which you do business, sports talk is a great icebreaker. It can be exactly what you need to start a conversation that bonds someone to you and ends with you getting the job, the client, or the next big order.

Discussing sports also can be an effective equalizer, giving you the chance to connect with someone you've never met, as well as a reason to connect again. However, women frequently don't know how to start this type of casual conversation, so instead they head right into the thick of negotiating. Believe me, it's easy to pick up a few sports-related tidbits on your car radio; or glance at the sports section of the local newspaper; or turn on *ESPNews* to get the quick-hit headlines of the day; or log on to one of the numerous sports sites on the Internet. Do you want to know how many people have been hired in business because they are alumni from the same school as their employer? That's called loyalty, and it happens in business all the time. You'll have a definite advantage with someone in a position to give you a job if you are able to "speak the same language," share common memories, and be a fan of teams from your mutual alma mater.

Honestly, you don't have to be a former player or sports fanatic to learn how to use sports as a tool for winning in your business. Anyone can be a winner by having faith, self-confidence, and the correct mind-set. Muhammad Ali has said many times, "It's lack of faith that makes people afraid of meeting challenges, and I believed in myself." Sounds awesome, doesn't it? You have the opportunity to practice success each and every day. Own it!

At nine years old, I walked into our kitchen in Far Rockaway, New York, and had a conversation with my mother, Renee, that changed my life. She told me that little girls didn't play sports, because it wasn't a ladylike thing to do, and that I would never make anything of myself if that's all I cared about. I looked at her, stood up, put my hands on my hips, and said, "I am going to make history. Get used to it."

I have no clue now where that assertiveness came from and how I found the chutzpah to say that to my mother, in *her* kitchen, at nine years old. But I can tell you that that was what was in my heart. And still is.

To be the best, and be perceived as the best—whether in sports or in business—you're going to have to face a lot of competition. I look back on my basketball career now and I can see that it has always been about execution. It's no different today: writing this playbook is an expression of my desire to share with you how to execute the winning plays so that you can consistently achieve high levels of success at whatever you choose to do in your life. Doing so brings me great joy and personal satisfaction. I was told a long time ago that if you have something good, you should share it with others. My life has been about dedicating myself to and accepting any challenge placed in front of me. Learning how to work well with others, help make them better, and not be afraid to fail, is what it's all about. No matter what happens in life, in business or on the basketball court, you must learn to execute in tandem with other people.

Often, success on the court requires a teammate doing the grunt work for you by setting the monster screen to get the shooter open. No job is too big and no job is too small. So ask yourself: Have you been there to help a coworker lately? Have you shared a great strategy or leadership skill with others around you? Do you give more than you take? Do you smile a lot? Working together and executing ideas as a team are critical to success in *any* business, not just sports.

We all have epiphanies in life. I had one in 1974 at 15 years old, when I was chosen to try out for the U.S.A. National Basketball Team. Forty women were flown in from all over the country to Albuquerque, New Mexico. Of those 40, only 10 would be chosen to attend a training camp under renowned coach Alberta Cox.

The second day of tryouts I had my ribs broken; the next day, I was on my way back to Far Rockaway. Coach Cox was sitting in the front seat of the car that was taking me back to the airport. From what I remember, she was from the Midwest—Missouri—and fairly stern. Now imagine me, a kid from Queens with my harsh New York accent (an accent that, later in life, I paid a speech coach $2,000 to teach me to lose, for a job at ESPN—true story!) So, we're in the car, and Coach turns to me and says, "Now, honey, we're going to need you in 1980, because you're going to be a very important part of U.S.A. basketball."

I looked at her and said, "Coach, you know I'm not real smart or nothin', but I do know '76 comes before '80, and I am going to be on the '76 Olympic team, so you'd better get used to me." (This conversation took place in 1974, so apparently I hadn't changed much from the day my mom and I had our conversation in the kitchen in Far Rock.)

Coach looked at me like I was crazy—as though she couldn't believe what had just come out of my mouth. But that's how I felt.

All the way back to New York, I was thinking, "How dare the coach of the U.S.A. National Team tell me what I *can't* be?" This woman should have been telling me what I *could be* and encouraging me, instead of taking my hope and my dream away.

At that point, Alberta Cox became the single most important person in my life, simply because she was the person who thought I *couldn't*. Even when I was tired, didn't feel well, wasn't motivated, didn't think I had it in me, I would go to the park and I would work, every single day. I would practice, over and over and over again, all of the things that I knew could make me better.

To be the best in business, you have to execute just like that— every single day. You have to deal with people in the field and in your office, with your clients, and your peers. Part of winning and using the lessons of sports involves encouraging others to be better than they ever thought they could be. You have to be the hope-giver; you have to empower people by motivating them to do things they didn't think they could do. You also have to teach them that failure is a noble trait, in business, life, and sports. We all are capable of trying to achieve something at a higher level when we are willing to take ourselves outside our comfort zone. In essence, we have to stretch the possibilities of who we are and what we can be.

A wonderful thing happened to me in July of 1976. At just 18 years old, and a senior in high school, I stepped up on a podium, bent over, and felt the amazing sensation of an Olympic silver medal being placed around my neck. I was, and to this day remain, the youngest basketball player in history—male or female—to win an Olympic medal. But my greatest satisfaction that day was running back to the Olympic Village in Montreal, grabbing the telephone off the wall, and calling Alberta Cox—collect—to say, "Coach, thank you! Thank you for making me more than I ever thought I could be."

Yes, it's important to have true belief and inner confidence in yourself, others around you might need to be encouraged by you, especially in a leadership capacity. Have you helped someone around you—perhaps a colleague in your office—become more than he or she thought he or she could be? It took somebody not believing in me for me to believe in myself. If I had listened to what Coach Cox had said to me, I might not be writing this book. She might have thought she was saying something positive to me at the time, like we will need you in 1980, but I took it as she didn't think I could make it in 1976.

I have a friend who used to say, "I'm the true champion of the world. I whipped Joe Frazier like I whipped George Foreman, like I beat Sonny Liston back in 1964." Many people know that friend as the greatest boxer of all time—Muhammad Ali. I still smile today when I remember him saying, "It's hard to be humble if you're as great as I am. If you're good, it ain't bragging."

We can all be great. We *all* have the ability. It helps, though, to have a playbook: to take the lessons learned in sports and apply them in our lives—at home, at work, even in personal relationships. I've dedicated my life to excellence and to empowering others by being a good leader—not just through words, but through the way in which I've conducted my life. I am consistent as a mom, friend, business leader, and athlete. I can be humorous, sarcastic, and sometimes even goofy, but I know when I have to be serious about what I do.

We are a society of goal setters. We want to be good at what we do, and we must always be willing to compete. Yes, ladies, it's perfectly acceptable to compete! And contrary to what my mother told me, it's *very* ladylike to win!

Even when you're good, don't be satisfied with yourself; realize that you can *always* be better. I tell this to business leaders and players all the time—even the best of the best, like Martina Navratilova, the greatest female tennis player of all time. When I trained Martina in 1981, she told me, "Nancy, I just want you to know, I had more wins last year than anybody on tour."

I replied, "Great. How many tournaments did you play?" She answered, "Twenty-five."

I then asked her, "How many did you win?"

She said, "Thirteen."

"And you're proud of that?" I asked. "If you play, you might as well play to win. Why don't you play 16 and win 13, instead of playing 25 and winning 13?"

Every time you walk out of your office, ask yourself, "How can I improve myself?" Be an inspiration, a shining light to anybody who crosses your path. That is *so* important as parents, coaches, and business leaders. It is our job to inspire and be the eyes of others who can't yet see the level they hope to reach one day. One of my favorite sayings is: *You don't know what you don't know.* If you expect the best from others, you must give them your absolute best. Each day is a new chance to inspire others around us; they see how we walk, talk, and handle the ups as well as the downs, how we face the difficult challenges. Have no regrets, and know that what you did, you did to the best of your ability.

Be Flexible: Don't Play the Play, Play the Game

Before we get into the heart of my *Playbook for Success*, there's one thing you must understand: You don't "play the play" in sports; you play the game. In other words, there might be something in your playbook that says, this is what we're going to do in this particular situation. But change happens, and you must be ready for it. You must be prepared and have viable options when change occurs. When someone takes away your best move, you need to have a countermove, or a plan B. One of the most valuable abilities you can have in business is to be flexible, so that you can adapt to the changing world around you. Yes, your playbook is your most important tool in being prepared, but it's a *guideline*. Don't adhere to your playbook so rigidly that you miss what's happening in the game. Otherwise, you risk having to make a lot of mea culpas.

Obstacles are actually opportunities, *if* you create a solid plan for success. I have found in both sports and business that if you have performed consistently well over time, you accumulate "excellence equity." Trust has to be earned when you are creating your team's plan for success. You do that by taking ownership of your decisions. Make decisions with confidence, then stand by them! Vision is a must-have. Do you have it in you? In many cases, people don't like to make decisions because they think, "What if I'm wrong?" Better to think, "What if I'm right?"

I got lucky about 21 years ago when my company, Events Marketing—which I started in Omaha, Nebraska—was putting on a tennis exhibition. I was bringing Martina Navratilova and Pam Shriver to play in the event at the Omaha Civic Auditorium. At a meeting I attended, which had been set up with some local business leaders, I was introduced to a young man named Howie Buffett. He worked for the City of Omaha at the time, and as we discussed my event and my vision for what it could do for the city—including giving 20 percent of the proceeds of the tournament to charity—I asked if he could help me find potential sponsors. I jokingly told him that if I wasn't able to get a title sponsor before Thanksgiving (which was two days away) I wouldn't be able to go back home to Dallas for the holiday—and I was a newlywed at the time. I also told him that I planned on staying in Omaha to cram in more meetings, since I didn't intend to leave until I found a sponsor.

As I was leaving his office, I turned to Howie, smiled and said, "Thank you for your time. I don't want you to feel any pressure to find a sponsor for me—although you'll be the cause of my divorce if you don't."

The next day, I was sitting in the home of my friends, Dean and Pat Thompson, when the phone rang. Much to my surprise, it was Howie. He said that he had told his dad we had met and that his dad wanted to invite me to Thanksgiving dinner with their family. I held my hand over the receiver, looked at the Thompsons, and said, "Remember that guy, Howie, I met yesterday? He says his dad wants me to come have Thanksgiving dinner with them."

They said without any hesitation, "Nancy, *go!*"

At this point, I'm thinking, "Dang, y'all don't want me to have dinner with you? I've been uninvited." But they set me straight, informing me of exactly who I'd be having Thanksgiving dinner with, if I accepted. "Nancy, it's *Warren Buffett.*"

I blurted out, "The singer, yeah. I know who he is."

Dean and Pat looked at me as though I was crazy. "No, that's *Jimmy* Buffett. *Warren* Buffett is one of the wealthiest, and nicest, people you will ever meet. Go!"

So of course I told Howie, yes, and thank you.

What a wonderful time I had: great dinner; warm, caring people—about six of us, including his family members. They made me feel so comfortable. To my surprise, Warren Buffett knew about my career, and me, and we bonded by talking about sports for most of the evening.

A few weeks later, Warren called and asked if he could play in my tennis event in a "celebrity doubles" match with Martina. I responded without pause, "Yes, of course." He played, had fun, and laughed at himself. And did I mention, his company, Berkshire Hathaway, bought hundreds of courtside seats, sponsored our VIP reception, and helped make our event a hit?

The fact that Warren wanted to play in our tennis event was awesome. He is incredibly knowledgeable about sports, and we have remained friends throughout the years. I've asked him many times since then, "Warren, why did you want to play in that tennis event with Martina?"

His answer never changes: "Because I admired the fact that when she was on top of her game—at a point when she had won Wimbledon five times, was number one in the world, and the best at what she did—she was still willing to change her serve to be technically even better." In other words, she was willing to keep fighting and working to be better *all the time*. This detail, and the fact that she is a kind, warm, and giving person, was never lost on Warren Buffett.

Warren recently invited me to his annual shareholders meeting in Omaha. Martina's name came up again as we were talking, and he said the coolest thing: "I only met Martina one time in Omaha, but I have always admired how she overcame obstacles and consistently worked hard to be great. I guess you would say she is a heroine of mine."

Wow! It doesn't get better than that. For Warren Buffett to hold a woman in such high esteem! He gets it. We all can earn that kind of respect. We *all* should strive to be somebody's heroine. Unfortunately, people have a tendency to behave like sheep; they like to hang together. They feel comfortable that way, because if an individual messes up, it's not obvious. They can hide in the crowd. And when somebody breaks away, the herd mentality says, "I don't like her. I can't believe she wants to be better than us."

Leaders, however, are different. They must have thick skins and be willing to stand alone until they can show others why they should follow them. You should therefore strive to adopt a leader's mentality: to be better and set the bar higher so that the person sitting next to you has to work harder to meet the standards you have set.

And as I said earlier, if you have something that's good, share it. As we used to say in school, "Don't hide it; divide it." Share with one another. Empower people around you to be better. It's really okay to want to be great, or better than your friends, coworkers, or teammates. It's okay to want to be the best. It *is* ladylike. You *can* have it all. So when people say, "Oh, you know, girls don't know how to compete," show them that, yes, we *do*. We really do.

Succeed Together!

There are more than 65 million women in the workforce today. Collectively, we earn over a trillion dollars. People with vision respect that. Way back in the nineties, National Basketball Association (NBA) commissioner David Stern said to me, "I would like to send you into 25 NBA cities to host working-women seminars. We want to attract corporate women as our fan base, and have them do business in the arena like men do. We think this is an area of growth and profitability for us, in terms of merchandising and ratings."

David knew how important women were to growing his future audience. He wanted to promote the league brand with women and girls because he knew that doing so would sell tickets and merchandise; but he also wanted to teach them how they could use the arena to conduct business the way men do.

So I went into 25 NBA cities, and we taught Basketball 101. No question was a bad question. Women in these meetings might ask me, "Is there a five-point shot?" I would explain, "No, but there is a four-point shot, if you make a three-point shot and get fouled and make your foul shot."

That experience was a good example of why it's important for women in many situations to talk to other women. That way, if you ask what's perceived as a "silly" question, you won't feel embarrassed or disrespected. It is also a prime opportunity to mentor one another, to empower the very people who need you most. Every day is an opportunity to teach and tutor!

Consider this, ladies: Who makes most of the decisions about which products end up in our homes? *We* do. Just ask my son TJ. He's a huge fan of mine, but not for being a Hall of Fame hoopster. If he wants something, he knows who he has to lobby! Who picks out the furniture? Mainly women. Guys may be responsible for choosing the La-Z-Boy recliner so they're comfy when they're watching the big game. (Now that's not a bad thing, because I like a good chair myself.) I think you get my point: We matter in a *big* way—and that translates into the power of the dollar.

When you see other people who are successful, who have made it to the top, it's very important not to feel something we call "HATERADE." *Support* the people at the top of the mountain; find out how they got there, how they became successful. Another great saying in sports that you can use in business: "Don't hate the player, hate the game." Better yet, find out how the game is played, so that you can become a contender yourself!

The players, the people who want to be successful, should be commended. On the way to the top, there are going to be a lot of naysayers. You've got to be strong, and you've got to be confident. You have to develop that lockdown mental toughness and make sure that you keep your eye on the bigger picture.

Accept All Challenges

I used to attend Michael Jordan's basketball camp in Chicago. On one particular day back in 1993, I found out that Michael was not only one of the greatest players of all time, but a great teacher as well. I was on the court giving a lecture to the camp attendees on a jab-and-go move. Out of nowhere, Michael walks onto the court and says to all the kids, "Today, Nancy and I are going to play one-on-one."

My first thought was, "You've got to be kidding me!" Why would he, my friend, want to humble me in front of 300 kids—not to mention *NBA Inside Stuff,* which was filming this event, as was some local media? NBA Entertainment, the production arm of the National Basketball Association, was there as well. I'm thinking, *why would Michael Jordan want to embarrass me in front of all these people?* I mean, he's a three-time NBA Most Valuable Player, three-time World Champion, and now he wants to play one-on-one against *me?*

This is where our game became an excellent teaching tool. The odds looked insurmountable for me, but when Michael came out on the court to play—the minute I accepted the challenge to play him—I automatically became the winner. How? I had to play at a higher level and maintain my sense of concentration and focus. It was *mano à mano*—if I might call myself a *mano* for the purposes of this discussion. In other words, I had to "come with the goods" against someone who was the greatest. I had to come with my best. You, too, have to come with the goods every day—no matter who you are or what business or market you're in.

So it was game on. My goal was to score and make his bald head sweat. I have honestly never played that well in my life or with the kind of focus I had that day on the court with Michael Jordan. When I tell this story to kids or adults, and ask them, "You want to know what the score was?," I wait for them to yell all kinds of one-sided scores back at me. Then I tell them, "Michael barely beat me. It was amazing. He won, 10 to 2."

Usually, the people I tell this story to start laughing (rough crowd!). But I tell them it was the two best points I ever scored. Because they were on *Michael Jordan*.

So often society tells you that if you have more money, you're a better person. If the scoreboard says you have more points, yours is the better team. But you know what? I had something far more valuable that day. I went out there and played better than I ever thought I could, and I was better for it. So, in reality, I *did* win, because I had improved. The lesson here is: Find the best people you can, and surround yourself with them. Always challenge yourself so you can push to the next-higher level. Each day, we have a chance to strive for intentional greatness.

It always helps to have a mentor or champion or someone who can help guide you to that next level. I've been fortunate to have had that someone many times in my life, in both sports and business.

Title IX Creates Equality

Women in business remind me somewhat of the notion behind the famous legal initiative called Title IX. Although a lot of people seem to have an opinion about Title IX, I always say that Title IX is not an opinion. It's a law. Affirmative action isn't an opinion either. It's a law. I often find that many women don't even know their legal rights!

Title IX is about opportunity and proportionality. It was enacted on June 23, 1972, and states that "no person in the United States shall, on the basis of sex, be excluded from participation in, be denied the benefits of, or be subjected to discrimination under any education program or activity receiving federal financial assistance."

It's probably no surprise that a lot of institutions are not in compliance with Title IX. Many businesses and corporations, for that matter, aren't in compliance either. As women, we need to give them a reason to hire us, trust us, and follow our lead. But shouldn't women who are qualified have an opportunity to freely move up the corporate ladder into decision-making and upper management positions?

After Title IX was enacted in 1972, over 90 percent of the head coaches for women's teams and about 2 percent of the coaches of men's teams were females. In 1970, just two years before the law went into effect, there were only 2.5 women's teams per school in all divisions. In 1978, the year of compliance, there were 5.61 women's teams per school. Thirty years later, in 2008, that number had risen to 8.65 teams per school.

Unfortunately many of these inequities graduate from college directly into the business world. We women are still in the initial stages of making our presence felt and appreciated in the business world. Far too many of us are still intimidated by the competitiveness, assertiveness, and self-assuredness of our male colleagues. We're flustered by the attitude a lot of men seem to display—that they have the *right* to succeed. In contrast, women seem to be constantly apologizing and asking permission for that right.

Why are men like this? *Because they played sports!* No one on a sports team *asks* for permission to hit a home run, apologizes for snatching the rebound, or behaves tentatively in *any* move they make. Yet that's just what too many women do.

Part of the problem is that before Title IX became a reality, few women had the opportunity to be a part of a team, to learn what it means to focus on winning, or to shrug off defeat, to strategize with people who are your friends one day and your opponents the next. I always ask moms and dads whether they support Title IX. One hundred percent of them should—that is, if they want their daughters, nieces, or granddaughters to have the same education and athletic opportunities in life as their sons, nephews, and grandsons. If you can't answer yes to that question, you have a lot of explaining to do to any young girl in your life!

I had (still do) the kind of personality that wouldn't take no for an answer. I forced my way into the world of sports, despite being told again and again that I didn't belong and "that's not what girls/women/*ladies* do!" Being able to leverage my experiences in the world of team sports has proven more valuable to me in the boardroom than any college degree I could earn. In *Playbook for Success* I want to share these skills with women who never had a chance to compete, or who, even if they did play sports when they were younger, have forgotten the important lessons they learned. They are the lessons of self-confidence, of believing in yourself, of making others around you better so that you—and they—are able to win at the highest levels.

As women, we must develop these skills if we expect to compete on a level playing field with men in the workplace. We need to hone these abilities if we're ever going to make up more than 2.8 percent of Fortune 500 CEOs or 6.2 percent of Fortune 500 top earners. We need these skills if we're ever going to fill more than 15.2 percent of Fortune 500 board seats, or if we're going to achieve success in the boardroom. These are skills we can use no matter where we are in the business world. They are necessary to provide us with the foundation to grow.

I *know* that sports are critical to success in the working world. I'm evidence of it. Under ordinary circumstances, I would not know Warren Buffett, Donald Trump, Kevin Costner, the late IMG super agent Mark McCormack, the Jackson family, and many others— incredible people in the business and entertainment worlds. It was sports that brought us together, that enabled us to form incredible friendships and develop trust.

Survey after survey shows that women at the top of their fields attribute their success in no small part to their early experiences playing team sports. Sports provided them with leadership skills, discipline, and the ability to function well as part of a team. One study from the University of Virginia found that *80 percent* of the top women in the Fortune 500 had played sports. These women cited their experiences in the sports world as having helped them succeed in the competitive corporate arena.

The connection between sports and success is undeniable: Women who competed are far more likely to be successful in the workplace. They have confidence, they learned how to improve their existing talents, and they know how to turn their weaknesses into strengths.

The proof is in the paycheck, too: 41 percent of the women surveyed in that University of Virginia study—physicians, lawyers and CEOs earning $75,000 or more—described themselves as "athletic," compared with just 17 percent of women overall.

So ask yourself, "Am I a hard worker? Do my coworkers believe in me? Can I communicate well with my colleagues, clients, and potential customers?" If the answer to any of those questions is yes, then this book will show you how to take those skills, expand them, and consistently use them to win the "championship game," the corner office, the CEO title, the seat on the board. On the other hand, if the answer to any of these questions is no, you *really* need to keep reading!

 **Plays to Remember**

- *Failure is noble.* Have the courage to come up with noble failures. This means being willing to try something new and to move outside of your comfort zone.

- *Be flexible.* Have a plan, but be open-minded, in case you have to use plan B. Be alert and ready for change.

- *Strive for intentional greatness.* Give your best *every day*, not just on the days you feel good. Don't get comfortable. Push yourself.

2

The Playbook

Luck is what happens when preparation meets opportunity.
—DARRELL ROYAL, UNIVERSITY OF TEXAS FOOTBALL COACH

The bible of any professional athlete, coach, CEO, or manager, and their teams is the playbook—a collection of policies, goals, and key plays. It's a compendium of the team's strategy, a plan for success, and a road map for winning. No professional coach, athlete, or business leader can function without a comprehensive playbook; and neither should you. In most cases, men have been given playbooks since the first team they joined. It's also an essential tool for women in sports or business, if they're going to compete to win.

Playbooks today are not just for athletes; political campaigns, businesses, and even entire communities use them. They function as a kind of global positioning system to help groups and individuals reach their goals. As Bill Parcells, former Dallas Cowboys coach and current Miami Dolphins executive vice president, has said: "He who doesn't have a map gets lost."

If you've been running your career ad hoc, with no clear path or playbook of your own, then you've been missing out on one of the most important components for success. Now and then, you might find intermittent success, or something you might consider to equate to success at the time. But to create truly consistent, positive results, you need your own *Playbook for Success*. It will make all the difference in sustaining improvement and obtaining your goals.

In this chapter, I explain what the *Playbook for Success* is, how to use it, and why it's so important—especially for women.

It's normally considered a privilege to receive a playbook, or be in the position to create one for your team. If you don't have access to one, then you're probably not a vital part of the team or the business. Conversely, being asked to return your playbook is not a good thing; it usually means that the team no longer needs or wants your services.

The playbook helps you lay the groundwork for success. The more information you have in it, the better you'll be able to take control and make the right choices at the right time. Sometimes, things aren't obvious until you write them down or lay them out visually. When you record and read the steps you want to take, and then study them, the actual moves—whether it's your approach for pitching an idea, making a sales presentation, starting a new job, or signing a new client—will eventually become second nature, whatever the business challenge.

The playbook should touch on all areas and cover every imaginable aspect of the business. The last thing you want to have to say to your boss, coach, or manager is: "I just didn't expect that," or "I had no clue." The playbook is created so that there won't be any surprises. It's there to help you understand your options, and so has to be put together with deep thought. In most cases, whoever is designing your team's playbook has experience in the area. I sincerely believe that you have to live the playbook and know what your team can do. A lot of this will, of course, depend on the personnel you have.

It's important to point out from the start, however, that no playbook is ever cookie-cutter, or applicable to every situation. Your company's *Playbook for Success* has to take into account every member of the team and his or her role on that team. That's why it's important to get to know each of your team member's strengths and weaknesses. If I have a team without good shooters, for example, then I need a playbook that concentrates on getting to the rim, using speed, applying defense, and generating turnovers—whatever our assets are. To have a successful game plan in your playbook, you have to know what your talents are as a team, and exactly what you are working with.

When creating the playbook with key teammates, you no doubt will be confronted with a variety of opinions within your leadership team. Behind closed doors, get those all out on the table. Allow everyone involved to voice his or her opinions and strategies. Then, once everything has been bantered back and forth, it's the responsibility of the coach, the leader, the decision maker, to take all of that information into account and make a decision. Just remember, when you leave that room, the meeting, the field, wherever you conduct your business, you must be unified in your game plan. My mantra has always been, "Agree, disagree, and align." Everyone must be on the same page when presenting a strategy to your team, and you have to be committed to the plan. Of course, you won't always be able to see what's coming. Nevertheless, a good playbook will give you the tools to deal with a variety of different scenarios. Budgets work this way, too, since they have built-in contingencies to give you flexibility. Your budget gives you a picture, a worksheet, and a plan that keeps you from spending all of your marketing dollars in the first quarter, for example.

When you're leading people, presenting a well-organized plan is a must. If you come across as disoriented or unsure, your employees are going to pick up on that—and the result can be divisive. Maybe your PowerPoint deck for your presentation could be a bit more concise, or you should address the client's needs a little more thoroughly. Putting something down on paper helps you to organize your thoughts and see clearly where you want to go. If you are confused internally, you are going to come across as confused externally, as well.

Successful Strategies for Your Team

When I coached the WNBA's Detroit Shock, it was the first time I created my own playbook for a team. I had been given many playbooks in my career, and now I had a chance to take those experiences and translate them into what I felt we needed in my first playbook. First and foremost, I kept it simple. Don't talk over people's heads. Keep your *Playbook for Success* easy—like the "Plays to Remember" that I highlight in the chapter conclusions throughout this book. The reason I'm such a big fan of keeping it simple is because it precludes the excuse: "I didn't understand."

One of the first times I appeared on ESPN's *NBA Fastbreak*, to comment on the Dallas Mavericks, I thought I had the perfect analysis. It went something like this: "He zipper-cut up and used the flare screen, and Dirk set a shake screen so the shooter got open and was able to make the shot because the defender was two slides to recovery." Well, *I* knew what I was talking about, and so did the guys with me on *Fastbreak*. But it wasn't such a good setup for the *viewer*. I made something that was so simple for me incredibly difficult for the viewer to understand.

Why confuse the people you work with by baffling them with your vast knowledge? Yeah, I'm a basketball maven, and you might be an expert business maven, but you need to communicate with your team and others on a level that enables them to clearly understand you and, ultimately, be successful. After my amazing analysis of that play, my boss, Bruce Bernstein, gave me some good feedback, in the form of the acronym KISS, which stands for Keep It Simple, Stupid. He reminded me to invite the viewer into my circle of knowledge through plain talk, and lose the jargon—or use it sparingly and explain what it means. And then explain again. Thanks, Bruce, for making me a better communicator.

I learned something valuable from that early broadcasting experience. It allowed me to grow and add that knowledge to my own personal playbook. It has become clear to me throughout my career that I hate to lose more than I like to win, but I can't deny that losing gives you a learning opportunity. When you win, it's great. You enjoy it. When you lose, I'm telling you, it grates on you for *days*. It never leaves your mind. You repeatedly ask yourself: How could I have been better? What could I have done to help my associates? Why did we lose the contract to another company? It's draining.

But, think about it, these are all relevant questions you would never bother to ask yourself had you won. Noble failures lead you to ask yourself the hard questions. Did everyone have the tools they needed? Did I communicate what was important? Did I keep it simple? Was the problem with strategy or effort? Skill or will?

When you win, it's all too easy to forget the learning opportunities while you're celebrating. It becomes all about the backslapping. Losing—or failing—gives you the chance to practice accountability and confront reality. Did you do a great job? Practice self-assessment and check your motives. I do that all the time. I ask myself if I'm doing things for the right reasons. Remember, when you're laying out this success plan, it starts and ends with *you*.

Your *Playbook for Success* should describe everyone's responsibilities in no uncertain terms, so that nobody can claim that they didn't know what they were supposed to do. It says, "Let's decide what we're going to do and commit to doing it." The goal can be to try for easy baskets, or to not make mistakes. It can be to build an organization that takes risks, or one that diversifies to avoid risks. Whatever your position, you must reiterate it. Tell your people what you expect them to do, on a daily basis. Give them tangible guidelines, and then let them work within those guidelines. I try not to micromanage those I lead. I believe it's important to give my team members space, to allow them to feel what they are encountering and make decisions on their own that are within the game plan. Of course, if you see someone consistently making the same errors, you will to have to address that with the person. But you don't have to do this after one occurrence. Take time to assess the situation.

Similarly, take time to "huddle up" before a big presentation. In other words, hold a team meeting with your staff. Go over the playbook again. Don't ever put yourself in a situation where someone can claim, "I didn't know that." Make sure *everyone* knows how his or her individual responsibilities contribute to the ultimate goal. Don't make people guess! And, I repeat, keep it simple; otherwise, people will forget. You've seen this in basketball games many times during the 30-second time-out. A player is getting ready to take a foul shot, so the whole team huddles up beforehand. It's little reminders like these that make the overall game easier for all the players. So get your group together before you run your play. Give them quick reminders before you walk into a meeting: "We have three things to concentrate on to stay on point . . ." The huddle can also be used for that last-minute rah-rah, *let's do it!*

In basketball, we have an approach we call *Time-Score-Possession*. If you know how much *time* is on the clock, and if you know the *score*, then you'll know which play to run. If you have a big lead and there's time on the clock, you can take a bigger risk. But if the score is close and time is running out, you can't take the extraordinary risks. If the play doesn't succeed, not only will you be giving the other team the ball, but you'll also be giving them momentum. In short, you will have just helped your opponent. In basketball, if you were losing momentum and the game was tight, I would hope that you would not take a quick shot if your team was not ready to rebound— especially early on the 24-second shot clock. I personally would want my team to be patient and work for something better, so that we could be successful and gain momentum in that situation.

Time-Score-Possession simply means being aware of your surroundings. Open your eyes and be alert. If you are rushed to get to a meeting on time and hustling to get a quick proposal or presentation together, take a breath. Regain your focus. You want to get the business and build the relationship, so it's best to keep it simple when you're getting your foot in the door. Execute, and gain their confidence. Once you're in the door, you're on the team. You're no longer on the outside looking in. Now you'll be able to show them exactly what you can do.

The Learning Plan

In basketball practice, we draw plays to help players remember how to execute them. Huddles last only about 30 seconds, at which point everybody's head is spinning with the multiple tasks they have to accomplish. Keep in mind that less is more. If we give someone 10 things to remember, he or she won't even be able to recall one. Give your team just two or three plays to remember at a time, and then communicate what you want. And *never* assume everybody is locked in. Case in point: When I was coaching in Detroit in 1998, in one game against the New York Liberty, we were up one point with six seconds left. New York had the ball in front of our bench, and I called time-out to tell my players how we were going to defend New York's last offensive play. I said to one of them, "Lynette, Vickie Johnson is a lefty and she wants to go left, so force her to the right." We break the huddle, Vickie catches the ball, drives left, and goes in for a game-winning layup with one second on the clock. I looked at Lynette, and shouted, "I told you, don't let her go left!" To which Lynette, responded, "Her left or mine?"

"Really?" I said to Lynette. (That's my favorite word for someone taking responsibility for his or her own actions.)

Again, don't assume anything. In this situation, my communication clearly had failed, with the proof right there on the scoreboard. Shortly after I pulled my hair out, I realized that not everybody remembers or understands what you say even when you think you have been clear and concise.

Hypothetically, if you are with your team and giving them strategy pointers, you might say:

- We need to grow our sales.
- Make sure the product is in the correct stores.
- Have you called all of our customers this week to see if they're satisfied?

Whatever the business scenario, make it dynamic, and give your team no more than three points to remember. You might want to illustrate these points both visually and verbally. I tell people what I would like them to do, and I show them as well. Then they do it. Hear it, see it, do it: I have found that's a great way to teach. One more guideline: Don't frame an order or directive as a question. Make it a statement.

The *Playbook for Success* is all about setting goals, determining your company's infrastructure, and making choices based on the personnel you have, to achieve optimal results. When I was in training for basketball, I always set goals. Some of those were physical, such as getting stronger or faster, or getting my body in shape. Others were mental, like knowing the offense and the defense and reading the scouting report. Still others were minigoals that led to bigger goals that in turn led to the ultimate goal— winning. The *Playbook for Success* gives your goals forward momentum and clarity. It's critically important when you're making choices to stay focused on each of those minigoals, from the beginning, and to follow through on your corporate strategy. Stay true to your beliefs. Your strength and conviction will have a lasting, positive effect on you and your team.

Sometimes staying focused is as simple as making a list to give yourself a visual of how to make progress. Check off the items on your list as you accomplish them. By doing so you'll gain momentum. Your team will respond to the synergy, too.

Your *Playbook for Success* is just that: a list, a plan for every single day, which strings together the minigoals in order to accomplish the ultimate goal.

Establish Your Leadership Style

My playbook includes a workout program, dress code, and a schedule of where everyone needs to be, when—just in case anyone is unclear of what is expected of them. Your playbook must create a team mind-set. It should include passion, commitment, and innovative thinking, to help others understand leadership and direction throughout their careers. The stakes in business today are higher than ever before, but the same principles apply. There's greater exposure out there in the business world because of the Internet, social networking, and all forms of electronic media. Nevertheless, you have to commit to your philosophies. Your playbook must serve as inspiration and a source of confidence and patience.

If I could have only one thing in this world, I'd ask for two: health and a good attitude. A good attitude allows you to reacquire anything you've lost. Bad attitudes suck the life out of people. You want to mirror success, so never slink into a room with your shoulders slumped. Come in with your shoulders back and your head high; walk with confidence and exude an aura of success. To get people to follow you, believe in you, and buy from you, you have to give them a reason and show them the way.

Body language is important. I say this all the time: If I can't see your teeth, you're not smiling. Little things like that have a substantial effect on others; people pick up on those clues. For example, I've been told that I walk confidently. It's a little thing, but people notice it. It's like Billy Crystal impersonating Fernando Lamas on *Saturday Night Live*, when he says, "It is better to *look* good than to feel good!" Looking good is part of the whole image of what you're selling to people. That's why we have a dress code in sports. The uniforms match. We wear the same color sneakers and wristbands. We had a dress code in Detroit. We were professional athletes. I recall once when we were leaving for a road trip, and one of our players was wearing linen and looked as if she had just stepped out of the clothes drier. I looked at her with tender, loving sarcasm and said, "Korie, really. An iron?" She told me she didn't have one. Then, in the spirit of finding solutions, I asked my assistant coach, Chris Collins, to buy Korie an iron and to remind her that this should never happen again. *Really.*

When you look professional, you act professional. We even rehearse our pregame warm-up. When attendees arrive to the game early to watch us warm up, they witness something so organized and structured it looks choreographed—because it *is.* The teams that are sloppy and can't get their pregame warm-up right—oh wow! It's a real predictor of outcome.

The same is true in business. If you're sloppy at the office and in your preparation, you are going to experience what we call "game slippage." Mistakes, from typos to major errors, will happen if you're not "on your game." We all have to help one another, and one way to do that is hold each other accountable to certain standards that we set and the impressions we create.

Every time I see Michael Jordan, he looks like he's going to a photo shoot for *GQ*, whereas the other guys are coming in workout clothes or warm-ups. I asked him once, "Why do you always dress up so nice in your *GQ* suit?" He said, "Someone might come through here and see me for the first time, and never see me again. This is the impression I want to leave with them." Michael Jordan gets it.

Life isn't going to be perfect. We all know that. There are days when you are going to be frustrated, and want to give up; but you can't broadcast that. Instead, take a look at yourself in the mirror and vow to work harder. Study your playbook. Your willpower to succeed will strike a chord with your organization, your team, your family, and the people with whom you are working shoulder-to-shoulder every day. Hard work is simply another test of your fortitude, so let your people see what you're willing to put in. Show strength and resolve.

If every one of your days has some element of drama in it, you're going to get caught up in increasingly more difficult days. You have to give people a reason to trust you and follow you. If your behavior is riddled with drama because you are focused on others—if you aren't consistent in your words and behavior—people are going to see that. If you expect your colleagues to be at the office at 8:00 AM, don't show up at 8:20. I always try to beat my players to the arena. I think it's important for them to see me there first. If I have a young player who likes to shoot around 3 hours before the game, I'm there 3 hours and 10 minutes before the game.

One thing too many people leave out of their plans and goals is the word "love." You have to find some love in what you do, or love the fact that you're going to make someone else better at what *they* love to do. I didn't love every coach I played for, but I loved that they kept me working to be better every day. Take the good that each person has to offer and leave the rest alone. Try to fall in love with what you do. It's so much easier to go to the office when you do!

The *Playbook for Success* is also about managing your time and energy. A lot of young people are coming out of college these days with high expectations of what they *should* earn and where they *should* be. They're providing wake-up calls to people in their thirties, who may well need them. These kids think they're smarter. They act like extensions of their computers. Their whole lives are saved in their phones. They are naturals at multitasking, and efficient at managing time, because they're always connected. That means the sooner the rest of us organize our time, the better. It's a lot like managing your finances: If you start saving early, you'll have more later. If you start organizing and setting goals early, you'll reach them sooner. Doing both will make retirement a lot more fun.

Don't Be Late. Really.

Time management starts with *being on time*. That means you. When you're an athlete, you sometimes learn this lesson the hard way. Show up late for the bus to the game, it leaves without you. Show up late to practice, you lose playing time. Time management is just as important at the office. Need to make copies before the meeting? Show up early and get it done. Too much work on your plate? Split it up.

Time management also requires that you find your pace. I have worked with people who actually think that they *can't* get their work done. One particular gentleman who worked for me, whom I'll call "the turtle," did his work, but couldn't seem to complete everything he was supposed to, on time, because he was so *slow*.

While "the turtle" was still planning, everything and everyone was moving and changing around him—and he was missing deadlines.

Time management also involves managing your time when you *aren't* at work, so that you are ready to roll each and every day. Like many athletes and coaches, I use a lot of sayings as motivation, and there is good reason for this: They help people understand—and they speak the truth. Here's a great one from football: "You can't make the club if you're in the tub." The same is true in business. You're not going to succeed in the office if you're in the bed. If you're frequently injured or late or sick, don't expect success to be waiting for you when you finally show up. If you're not at work, someone else will be; and then you'll be responsible for giving someone an opportunity for taking your job. You are in control of the label, "She's lazy." Never let that be associated with you, by anyone.

Just ask Wally Pipp, the New York Yankees first baseman in the 1920s. As the story goes, Pipp asked to sit out during a game on June 2, 1925, because he had a headache. A young man by the name of Lou Gehrig went in for Pipp, thus kicking off Gehrig's legendary streak of 2,130 consecutive games. Gehrig went on to be called "Iron Horse" for his strength and dependability. His record held for 56 years, until Baltimore Orioles shortstop and third baseman Cal Ripken, Jr. broke it when he played his 2,131st game on September 6, 1995. Cal was likewise called baseball's "Iron Man" because he showed up for work no matter what injury was dogging him. He played an additional 502 straight games over the next three years; his streak finally ended at 2,632.

These are both great illustrations of why it's so very important to show up! Lou Gehrig took his spot at first base and went on to own the record for 56 years. Remember this story, ladies, and use it to your advantage in the boardroom or in a staff meeting if you have a problem with commitment on your team. You better believe Lou Gehrig and Cal Ripken were committed. When you're dealing with someone who's not, pull out your Wally Pipp story and get ready for the guys in the room to look at you and wonder, "How does she know about Wally Pipp?" Don't get me wrong; I'm not saying you need to know every baseball, football, or basketball statistic. You just need to know some key stories, and when and how to use them.

"You can't win the Kentucky Derby with a donkey," a man named Richard Head once told his daughter when she was new at coaching and trying to build her team. That woman became the winningest coach in National Collegiate Athletic Association (NCAA) history: the University of Tennessee's Pat Head Summitt, who has won a record eight NCAA titles—second only to the great John Wooden of UCLA, who won 10 NCAA men's titles. The people who work for you—your personnel—are everything, it's true. In sports and in business, you're only as good as your teammates, the people who play with you and for you. Surround yourself with fierce competitors and you'll be able to contend on a higher level. That's why athletes tend to be such great hires in many cases. It doesn't matter if they're role players or superstars; they are willing to compete day in, day out. They have been taught not to be the weakest link and to have high standards and good fundamentals.

Loyalty Matters

When I interview people for a job, I often start by asking them how they define loyalty. You can find out a lot about people when you ask that question, and you'll be astounded at the different perceptions people have of loyalty. Listening is a skill, a lost art if you will. For example, when you're interviewing people, you're supposed be the listener, not the talker. It's not always about us; it's about *them*. Who are they? What do they think? What has been their previous experience? What do they expect from you, your company?

If you're looking for information about your candidates, it doesn't hurt to Google them. Then you won't have to say later,

"Oh, well, I didn't know she was recently let go by our competitor. I asked a lot of questions, but she never brought it up." There are a lot of ways to gain insight into people today. We can look at stats, call coaches, and look at film to see if a player fits our style and system. Call people. Conduct due diligence and find out what you need to know.

The more you're around people, the more you'll begin to notice behavior patterns and understand how to get results out of them. Different people take different journeys to the same destination. Your *Playbook for Success* allows you to track those various journeys, and prepares you for the unexpected.

Once you have hired your team, you have to take care of them. The first year I coached in Detroit, I was the only coach in the league who didn't get a technical foul (commonly referred to as a "T"). I thought that was a good thing; I soon realized that my players needed to know that I would stand up for them every step of the way. Doug Collins, who was coaching the Detroit Pistons at the time, told me, "Go upstairs and have an addendum put into your contract to have the team pay for your first 25 technical fouls of the season. Then use them. Let your team know you're in their corner."

So I did. And the next season, I used my technical fouls. The first time I went up to the ref and asked her to give me a "T," she said, "Are you sure? You haven't done anything!" I said, "I know, but I need it, and I need it now." She gave me the "T"—and the team thanked me. (Of course, I didn't let them know I had asked for it!) This was another important lesson for me: I learned to generate loyalty by taking care of my people.

You have to show your people that you are willing to take some heat for them in business, too. You can do it in small ways and in big ways. Don't be cheap. Spend $500 more a year on lunches. Don't have alligator arms that can't reach into your pocket or that nice Gucci pocketbook. Don't be the accountant at the table, the one who says, "There are six of us, so let's divide it."

Pick up the dang check once in awhile. It will come back to you a hundred times.

Likewise, involve yourself with the people you're working with; become a part of what's going on in their lives. Never forget: Your assistants can make or break you. They have to want to set you up for success and help highlight your strengths. They hold the cards, so they better "get it." They must be protective of you and proactive for you and your time, and be two steps ahead of you— taking care of the little things, keeping your life and schedule organized, handling the items you don't have the time for. That is managing effectively, which better organizes and helps you.

If you have young people on your team—rookies—give them responsibilities, and then show them the way. In most cases, young people have the energy and want to make the effort. But they need direction. Help them. Let them know you're all in this together, and that there's no job too big or too small—all the way to the top.

You want loyalty, so show loyalty. *You must trust.* If I were going to take a job tomorrow selling medical devices, for example, I would surround myself with the people who know that industry and the company. Or if I were taking a coaching job in the Atlantic Coast Conference (ACC), I would hire an assistant who knows that league. Then I would place my trust in that individual. Hire people who know others in the industry and the business, who understand the rules and procedures, and who can help you become aware of what's in front of you. Hire people who have traveled the market and know the reps, then trust them. Don't be threatened by them.

Athletes have to develop a thick skin. Our playing time is determined by our ability and our impact. But our minds can be a terrible hindrance, because we invent scenarios that aren't real: "I didn't get invited to the board meeting [or get the new client], because my boss doesn't like me." As a manager, leader, or a coach, you'll spend 80 percent of your time addressing personnel issues because you're dealing with people, and people are fragile. Always go back to your playbook.

It's not my job to take away a player's innate ability to play. If it works for you and the team, it's not my job to take away your skill at selling or creating. My job is to eliminate some of the unpredictability by laying out the plan, teaching the fundamentals, demanding teamwork, and inspiring success. By no means am I saying you will never have to fire, trade, or reassign someone. It will happen. It's part of life and business, and can be very emotional at times, especially if it's a friend.

It can be lonely for women at the top, but a leader doesn't deserve the title unless she is willing to stand alone sometimes. I've done it; in fact, I'm doing it now. I was the only woman to play in a men's professional league with the United States Basketball League (USBL) in 1986 and 1987. Today, I'm the only woman to coach an NBA men's Development League team for the Dallas Mavericks, in Frisco, Texas. You must be strong to do something like this—mentally strong, confident, and fearless. Women get pigeonholed into gender-specific roles. Guys sell, and girls handle the customer service side of the business. It doesn't have to be that way. When women are armed with the right skill sets and attitude, they can experience success in any role.

And, sometimes, you have to be willing to push the envelope, to give yourself those breaks. It's important for women to recognize that adaptability and flexibility create opportunities. For example, I've never stuck to a single position in basketball. I played center in high school, then moved to power forward on the USA team. I was a forward during my first year at Old Dominion University, but the last three years, I was asked to play point guard. What were the common denominators of all of those positions? Winning, leading, and a willingness to try other positions so that I could expand my game. I dig the fact that coaches coach, but it's players who win the games. Sometimes you have to be willing to be adventurous, to get out of your comfort zone. Too frequently, we women don't let ourselves off of this predetermined track of what we're "supposed to do." You have to be willing to change your behavior, and even to be uncomfortable, at times, to be successful.

You can't let fear paralyze you and create inner doubt. You have accountability; so do others. You must instead focus on what you can control. I can't help it if one of my players stays out all night or gets a DUI. He or she will have to deal with the consequences of his or her decisions. I do have to be prepared to manage and offer solutions for everyone else around me. Again, go back to your playbook. See who's on your depth chart. Have you been developing other people, or have you focused solely on your "star" employees? I learned a long time ago that it's ideal to maintain a balance of experience and youth. Youth pushes experience, and experience is the eyes of youth. When you can develop those two in combination, they motivate each other to be better.

Fortune 500 companies don't break sales records with newbies. They do it with people who have a wealth of experience. I have found that people who work together and play together develop strong relationships and can help each other be more successful. Take advantage of people you connect with. Go to meetings. Shake hands. Get the tip. Buy the dinner. Most importantly, ask questions and learn the business. Take advantage of the opportunities: be in the right place at the right time, ask for help, listen, and learn.

You don't win championships with a team of only rookies. Though they may be fearless and full of energy, they are not experienced enough to be consistent. Without doubt, young people are a great asset for your organization. They keep the veterans who have settled into their "I'm really good and successful and have the car and the house" mode on their toes. They remind those people to look over their shoulders. It makes them a little edgy to have the young Lou Gehrigs around; it motivates them to work harder.

I'm all about competition, and you should be, too. The minute you're satisfied with your performance, you let the competition surpass you.

Plays to Remember

- *The playbook.* This is your organized map to success. Commit to it.

- *Really?* I believe in the potency of loving sarcasm. A little goes a long way. "Really?" is one of my favorite ways to use it. Really is *my* word. It's about accountability and putting the responsibility back on the responsible party, without a lot of nagging and lecturing. "You're 15 minutes late to the conference call. Really?"

- *Agree, disagree, and align.* It's important to give everyone an opportunity to put everything out on the table during meetings. You'll agree and disagree, but when you walk out, you all have to be aligned and moving in the same direction—toward success.

3

Find Your Love and Passion

I don't know what my limits are, but I can tell you right now that I'm not afraid to find out!

—NANCY LIEBERMAN

hy did Michael Jordan return to basketball twice after retiring? Why did I come out of retirement at age 39 to play with the WNBA's Phoenix Mercury? Why did I do so again at the age of 50 and risk my legacy to play just one more game with my old team, the Detroit Shock? Why was Tiger Woods able to play one of the best rounds of golf of his life to date with two stress fractures and a torn knee ligament? Why did Courtney Paris promise to return her four-year scholarship to Oklahoma University if she didn't lead the women's basketball team to the 2009 NCAA championship?

In a word: love.

Finding your love is the first step to creating your *Playbook for Success*, because if you love what you do, you'll have the passion you need to succeed. Sure, the best players are getting paid a lot of money for playing now, but they started playing as kids just for the fun of it and because they loved what they were doing.

The same holds true in the business world. Without a fire in your belly to compete and do your work to the best of your ability, mediocrity will rule. You can't achieve your goals if you can't articulate your dream. You articulate that dream in your playbook.

Passion is what enables someone to walk an 18-hole golf course lined with millions of fans while in excruciating pain and *still win*. Passion is, as former First Lady, Lady Bird Johnson, once said, "Becoming so wrapped up in something that you forget to be afraid."

If you don't absolutely love what you're doing, every day—whether it's running the company, practicing law, or selling computers—then get out of it and find something else, because you will never be "successful" in the fullest sense of the word. You might think you're doing well for a while, but when things get tough—personally, professionally, or economically—your lack of passion will come back to haunt you, and you will fail.

This is the first play I teach in the *Playbook for Success*, and it's really the most important one. By looking deep within yourself, asking and answering questions, and reflecting on your past achievements and failures, joys, and sorrows, you can master the play of identifying your love and passion. Once you have that, you can extend it into the workplace in your quest for a win. You won't have to say much; those around you will pick up on your drive and your enthusiasm, and it will be contagious.

One word of caution before I continue here: This chapter may serve as a wakeup call that the job you're in may not be the right one for you—simply because you do not have enough passion to take you to the top. The legendary UCLA Coach John Wooden once said, "We're not born in the same environments, but we're all absolutely equal in having the opportunity to make the most of what we have. . . ."

Toughen Up—Mentally

When I was training Martina Navratilova, she called me from the Australian Open to tell me that she had pulled her hamstring and couldn't play. She was upset that she was hurt, and wanted to pull out of the event. But in tennis, as in many other sports, you play for the majors, and this was a major. So I asked her, "Are *you* hurt, or does *it* hurt? If you're hurt, then you leave the tournament and go home to see a doctor. If it hurts, then get some treatment and go out there and play." Sometimes you have to be able to play through pain. It's mental. You're tired, and you're griping because so much is coming at you, and you think you can't do it anymore—but you can! You have to push over the threshold to reach your full capacity. After receiving treatment from the trainers, Martina went on to win the Australian Open that year. (Thank goodness she called me!)

I believe successful women have to be competitive and decisive. We have to have love, passion, vision, and a game plan attached to that passion. Men are taught to win from the day they are handed a ball and a glove. Women are taught to "play nice" so that everyone will be happy; therefore, they're more concerned about being liked. You can't worry about that. It may sound cold and disconnected, but if you spend your life worrying about what people think of you, those people will pass you by on their way to the top.

The Women's Sports Foundation did a study comparing the experiences of boys and girls. Consider this scenario of a young girl learning how to dive from her parents. Mom and Dad are sitting by the pool and little Susie stands at the end of the diving board. She puts up her arms, bends over, dives in . . . and does a belly flop. She falls flat on her face and stomach—smack!—like almost every kid the first time they dive in a pool. Dad says, "Nice try, Susie!" and goes over and pulls her out of the pool. Susie is crying, so Dad wraps her in a towel, hugs and kisses her, and tells her how great she did and then sends her over to Mom to be loved and nurtured.

Now consider the same experience for little Johnny; it's a bit different. Johnny goes to the end of the board, gets ready, and does a belly flop just like Susie. He too cries after he hits the water so hard, but when Dad goes over to pull Johnny out of the pool, he says, "Son, get back up there. Let me tell you what you did wrong." Or, even, "Let me *show* you what you did wrong."

The Women's Sports Foundation study concluded that boys get three instructions for every one that girls receive. Boys are taught to get back up on the horse—again and again. Women typically have to learn this lesson as adults, because we often aren't taught it as children. But you'd better believe all the boys got this message—

loud and clear. Women also have to learn not to take it personally when we are corrected, or believe that we can't afford to get things wrong. We have to harden up and develop a sense of tough love for ourselves, for what we're really trying to do to be successful.

Michael Jackson's Message: Man in the Mirror

I'm going to get personal for a minute. As you know, I'm passionate about my career in sports and business, but more than anything, I love being TJ Cline's mom. TJ is my son, and each and every day I get a chance to influence his life. I want to be TJ's role model and hero in life.

Let me give you an example: TJ was in the house with me on June 25, 2009, when we heard that Michael Jackson had died. My son could see that I was deeply affected, and he wanted to know why.

This gave me the opportunity to share and teach TJ about giving and helping others to be better. There are people who cross your path in life and who leave an indelible mark on you. The Jacksons have been friends of mine since I was 25 years old, and losing Michael was really hard on me because he and I are the same age and we had a lot in common, personally—notably, we both had difficult and painful relationships with our fathers in our childhoods. Despite his upbringing, this musical genius had the most amazing love and passion for entertaining and caring about other people. I think you'll agree with me that it wasn't until Michael passed that many people finally stopped to think, wow, he was the genuine article, completely authentic. Listen to the words in his songs and look at the things that he did. Nobody who's "cheap" gives $300 million dollars to charity, okay? That is philanthropy.

The day of Michael's funeral, I was thinking, as we stared at his coffin at the Staples Center, here lies this tremendously, fabulously talented, kind, genius of a human being, who really did try to change the world and make a difference.

Do *we*?

Yes, he was different, and he accepted being different; but it hurt him. He clearly faced a lot of critical judgment. Sadly, when someone isn't like us, people too often are quick to mock that person because his or her differences make them uncomfortable. In spite of this, Michael never lost his passion for what he did on a daily basis. He had the most amazing innocence, a childlike love of his "job," even as he got older.

Believe it or not, you have a chance to do that, too. Every day that you're out there, every day that you're trying to be a leader or a champion, you're going to be judged. But that's when the fun begins, because none of us, not even Michael Jackson, can take it with us. As far as I know, the houses, the cars, and the money—none of that went into the coffin with him. You know what was there? The message he sent to all of us, one that resonates even more in death than it did in life. Why? Because we took this young man for granted. None of us wants to be taken for granted. We all want to be appreciated. Everything else we acquire in life—all the creature comforts and money—is on the loaner program. So make sure to share what you have, wisely. We aren't taking it with us, so the way we share—including mentoring and helping others—will be our legacy.

We're living and we're breathing, and right now, people depend on us. That's what champions are about. You don't know how far you can go until you go too far. How many of you go too far in your business each and every day? How many special few really do that? It's all about quality over quantity.

As I mentioned in Chapter 2, I have just taken on a very daunting and challenging responsibility as the head coach of the NBA's Development League (called the NBA D-League) team for the Dallas Mavericks. Not only will I be making history, but I also know I'll be facing a fair amount of pressure and judgment, because I'll be in the spotlight as a woman coaching men. I know I'll have to guide, lead, build character, teach and tutor, and shift players' comfort levels and their behaviors. I'm excited about that. I and my colleagues will have an opportunity to affect the lives of not only the players but also our entire franchise, from top to bottom. We will be invested in each other's lives. Everyone, from our general manager to ticket sales personnel, will know that we value and appreciate their hard work and effort. If they need guidance or help, they will get it, in abundance. We are a team, on and off the court. We will play to each other's strengths, and no one will feel abandoned or un-appreciated in his role on our team.

I don't know what my limits are, but I can tell you right now that I'm not afraid to find out!

Rucker Park: The Little White Girl Plays with the Best

Growing up as the "little white kid"—the "little white *girl*"—playing basketball in Harlem, I didn't know my limits then, either. Love of the game is what got me past what others around me saw as limitations. As an 11- and 12-year-old, I would take the train 50 minutes from Far Rockaway (Queens) to Harlem, to play basketball at famed Rucker Park—at night.

The park is named after Harlem teacher Holcombe L. Rucker, who started a basketball tournament there in 1950 to encourage street kids to aim for college careers. You may have seen it in the AND1 Mixtape Tour. It's where all the legends of the game (among them, Wilt Chamberlain, Kareem Abdul-Jabbar, Julius Erving, Allen Iverson, Joakim Noah, Rafer Alston, and many more) came to play and make their reputations—including this little white girl. Even as a kid, I knew I had to play against the best to be the best.

I'd get on the train, taking extra T-shirts with me to shove them into my jacket so I would look bigger. At the time, I used to talk kind of like this: "Yo, you gotta problem with me? What's your prob-lem?" With this attitude, I'd walk into Rucker Park and all the guys would look at me, and I'd look back at them like I belonged there, and say, "Like, who's got next? Because if you don't have next, I have next and I'm going to be shooting over there. So if you want to play, you need to come see me."

These guys would look at me like, "Who's the little white girl who's acting like she owns Rucker Park?" And you know what? My attitude cut through a lot of social issues for us, because we found out that even though it looked as if we didn't have a lot in common, we had *everything* in common. We all wanted to play, and we all wanted to win. We all loved this game and wanted to stay on the court.

Those guys taught me trust; even though I had never met some of them, the minute we became teammates, we knew we had to trust each other, and we had to believe that we could make each other better, if we intended to win. Later, they started riding the train back to Far Rockaway with me, so that nothing would happen to me on the way home. African-American boys from Harlem and the little white Jewish girl from Far Rockaway became equals because we had formed a bond, established trust, and had respect for one another. Bottom line: This happened because we had the same *love*—basketball.

Muhammad Ali's Gift of Hope

I will never forget all the myriad ingredients that came together to help me overcome adversity. There were no scholarships when I was coming up through high school. Title IX was just starting, back in the early seventies. Fortunately, for me, there was this one particular man.

I was watching TV one day, and there was this guy saying, "I'm the champion of the world. The odds were against me, but I'm too pretty not to be the champion of the world." I was like, "Oh my gosh! This guy is on TV saying he is the greatest of *all time*." From that day forward, from the time I was 10 years old, Muhammad Ali was my hero of heroes. He taught me I could be anything that I wanted to be, if I was willing to put in the time and the effort to become who I wanted to be. Talk about passion. *He* had passion.

Now, again, how could I have anything in common with Muhammad Ali? But as with the guys on the court in Rucker Park, we had *everything* in common. Ali's confidence, vision, and passion gave me the direction to head to become who and what I wanted to be. Thanks to him, I set my personal goal at 10 years old: to be the greatest female basketball player of all time.

Things just don't happen for you. You have to make them happen. I was a poor kid from a one-parent family growing up in New York City, and I didn't have it easy. I remember that the heat and electricity were constantly being turned off in my house. I recall, too, my mother dumping out her purses and scrounging around for change to put gas in the car, so that we could go find my father to get our child support payments.

My point is, do not let your environment, your situation, or other people hold you back from what you want to be and do. You are accountable for who you are, for what you are, and for what you want to be. As for me, I spent nights playing in the schoolyard until 8:00, 9:00, and 10:00, whether it was snowing or raining—it didn't matter. It would be so dark out in the schoolyard that we called it "radar ball." We played by moonlight. We could see the glint on the rim and hear the ball bounce, but if the ball rolled too far away, we had to come back in the morning to find it. It didn't matter; we just wanted to play.

You couldn't get me out of the park. I was always there working on my game. My mom would come to the corner and yell at me to come home for dinner, and my response was always, "Ma, just one more game." She never had to kick me out of the house to go practice; she was always trying to get me to come back in the house! All those days taking the train to Harlem to play against the best, all those nights and days in the schoolyard—I was taking responsibility for my own path.

And as I've said before, women have to get over the fear of failure. Listen to Lady Bird: doubt paralyzes. I've seen so many people fall short of achieving true greatness simply because they were afraid to fail. To me, fear is about the unknown. You don't know what's there, so there's doubt and insecurity. But if you live at a higher level, you come to regard the unknown as an opportunity—something presented to you that not everyone gets.

Here is an example: In 1980, I was the number one draft pick of the Dallas Diamonds in the first women's professional basketball league. Though I knew I was going to the Women's Basketball League (WBL), at the time I was playing at Xavier High School in New York City's West 16th Street—a girl playing in a men's league. When I got home one night, I got a call from Jerry West, a Hall of Famer and former general manager of the Los Angeles Lakers. He says, "We'd love for you to come to LA and play for the Lakers in our summer league." So I fly to LA and go to my first practice with these dudes.

Here I am, a 22-year-old, 5-foot-10-inch, 150-pound chick playing with these giants. The coach of the summer league was Pat Riley, and it was his first coaching opportunity. Every time we got into a practice, he would tell us what the drill was going to be. If he said, "Let's run an 11-man break. Who knows how to run it?" I'd stick up my hand and say, "I know how to do it, Coach." Now, I'll tell you, at that time, I had no *idea* how to run an 11-man break drill. But I wasn't afraid of giving it a try. No one else there would raise their hand, because they didn't want to end up looking bad. I didn't know how to do it, but I knew I'd do something, and he would correct me as we went along.

In the fall of 2007, Pat Riley was inducted into Basketball Hall of Fame. That summer, I got a phone call from the Miami Heat, where Pat had coached since 1995. They said they were producing a video for the Hall of Fame induction dinner and that Pat had given them a list of people he wanted to appear on the video, and I was on it. I was surprised: *Why me?* When I saw him two months later at the Hall of Fame, I approached him and after I said "Congratulations!" I asked, "So, how come you wanted me on your video?" Pat told me that I had been important to his career. Well, I can tell you, I was stunned. He told me, "You taught me not to be afraid of anything."

You never know when you're going to have a teaching moment. Back in 1980, in the LA summer league, I had just been doing what I loved. I didn't want to be known as a girl playing in the men's league; I just wanted to be known as a player. That was my goal.

I think you see my point: Try not to worry about being the only woman CEO or VP, or the only female on the board. Just be who you are and contribute, because you never know who you might be inspiring along the way.

The Power of a Woman's Natural Traits: Empathy and Intuition

A valuable natural trait women have at their disposal and can use effectively in business is empathy. Empathy is not that far removed from love on the emotional IQ chart. For example, I once played through an injury during a 2010 celebrity exhibition game in Phoenix. (My stilettos had done me in at the NBA All-Star events in Dallas a few weeks earlier—I totally wrenched my knee. (True story!) After that game, I had a meeting with a potential new client, Gregg, to discuss my giving business leadership speeches all over the country. Even though I was hurting, tired, and sore, I sat down with Gregg and we started talking about his background. He told me he had raised four kids on his own, so I told him about my son, TJ Shortly thereafter, the conversation swung toward sports and the game I had just played in, wrenched knee and all. (Gregg had been kind enough to attend the game, to watch me play.) We then began discussing sports in general. On the basis of this common interest, we connected, and I'm confident we'll do business together in the future.

It's okay to build relationships with the people in your office, or the people you're pitching or selling to. You *want* to find ways to connect. It brings you closer, because they know you care. Women are nurturers by nature, and we should use that tendency to our advantage.

I am very much a nurturer with my team. I don't sit at the front of the plane or the bus with management. Instead, I pick a player and sit with him or her, and we might never talk basketball. I'll ask, for example: "How's your boyfriend?" "How's your girlfriend?" "Is your grandma still sick?"

Get to know the people around you. Build those relationships. Give your colleagues and teammates a big pat on the back, send them a "great to see you" email or text message. Something that simple can pull somebody up on a day when they need it. Successful moms, businesswomen, and coaches do this, and it gives them a head start in dealing with their kids, clients, associates, coworkers, potential prospects, and players. As a matter of fact, each weekday, my buddy, NFL great Deion Sanders, sends a text—a positive, spiritual message—to start the day. I look forward to it so much that, honestly, when he doesn't send one, I call him up and say, "Where's the message?" They're little notes, like: "Serve others." "Make other people better." It changes my outlook each day and gives me a focus.

Another powerful asset that females possess (when they pay attention to it) is their intuition. Stay away from the "shoulda-coulda-woulda" dance. Then you won't ever have to look back with any regrets. Do what your gut is telling you. When you don't act on your instincts, you're probably afraid, and you don't trust your choices. Be decisive. Don't get caught up in "maybe." Intuition and instinct are fine, but, ultimately, it's all about yes and no. As Yogi Berra said, "When you come to a fork in the road, take it." Being competitive is about being decisive. Say: "I'm running this play." "We're going after this client." Not: "Well, I think . . ." Say, "I believe," and "We *must*." Base your decisions on your ability to take action. Don't worry if you're right or wrong, as long as you have thought out what you plan to do in advance and your decision is clear-cut.

Mentoring and Creating Opportunities for Others

In 26 years, I've had about 75 interns. As I was coming off the air one night after a Dallas Mavericks game, one of them, Collin, who had interned for me in Omaha, Nebraska, 20 years ago, came up and thanked me for mentoring him. He had been a great intern, and I have no doubt he's doing well today. When I saw him, he was so excited, and wanted to introduce his little boy to me. It was so cool. I had given him the opportunity to gain experience in a work environment and learn from it. It was satisfying to see him all those years later. It felt so good.

When you love something, *really* love it, you want to share it with others. Three good ways to do that are to mentor, teach, and tutor. It's so important to put your fingerprint on the future in this way. I try to do this every chance I get. It's the little things that bring people together; that's what mentoring is about—sharing what you love. Sharing a smile, a story, or putting someone in the moment. We want to create those moments for others, to enable them to imagine what *can* be, what they *can* do, that they can indeed become successful. You share what you know on different levels. You show it consistently, again and again. Mentoring is a daily show of action.

Negotiating 101: Why Should I Have You on My Team?

It can be hard to say no to a woman. We can be relentless when we are passionate about something. Understanding this can help you when you are negotiating to get your desired results. "Coach, I know it's the end of the game, but I can run that play if you just give me a chance. I'll show it to you." *That's* negotiating. When I was playing, I always tried to convince my coach that I could continue to play even with three fouls. It became my standard line: "I can play with three fouls, Coach. I know I can do it. I won't get my fourth." I was always negotiating, even at that young age.

It's important for women to know how to negotiate skillfully, without using emotion, but by presenting what I call "the meat." Why should I pay you more? Why should I have you as part of a team? Give me reasons. Using emotions to negotiate is a trap, because you're not showing what you can do. You have to demonstrate exactly what you offer, why it's valuable, and why you deserve the raise, the job, or the promotion. Present a valid reason. It's not about playing time or getting in the business game; it's about money, your bonus, your skill set, or your promotion. You have to be believable, trustworthy, honorable, and capable of doing the job in order to negotiate well. I hone my negotiating skills every day with my son. I tell him, "I'll play you two out of three games of ping pong. You win, I'll clean your room. You lose, you clean your room, and more." I try to make it fun by adding the sports element.

When it comes to negotiating for money, it goes back to asking. When is a good time to ask for a raise? Well, never. It's like the guy who doesn't want to break up with his girlfriend before her birthday. There'll always be an excuse. You have to *make* it a good time if you want something. It's important to do your homework and be prepared. Know everything you can about the person making the decision on your raise or bonus. Know everything you can about the company, where it stands financially and what it needs to do to improve that standing. Then go in there and give them a reason to *want* to pay you what you're asking.

When I came to Dallas in 1981 to play for the Dallas Diamonds, I wanted $100,000. Dave Almstead, the general manager at the time, told me that the top player on the team was making only $35,000, and asked me how he could justify a contract at that amount for me. I told him that I was the best player in the country (as you can see, I was very humble). I also told him that if I could bring in 3,300 people a game, at $7 a ticket—plus generate valuable media attention—it would be more than worth it to him. The year before, Dave's team had averaged 1,100 people a game.

It was—worth it to him. The media gave the team exposure it couldn't afford to buy. We averaged more than 3,500 attendees a game and received a significant amount of attention from the media. I averaged 26.3 points per game, and the Diamonds went on to the WBL finals, before eventually losing the best-of-five series to

Nebraska. I had laid out a game plan. I didn't ask for favors; instead, I told Dave what I believed I could do for him. It was far from a sophisticated approach, but what mattered was that I delivered on what I had negotiated.

When I accepted the job in Frisco, Texas, with the NBA, I didn't need to be the highest-paid coach in the Development League. I recognized that I brought valuable elements to the overall business plan that, in most cases, coaches of other teams simply couldn't:

- It's historic to have a woman coach a men's team.
- I have lived in Dallas for 30 years and have long-term relationships with businesses and sponsors in the region, and families there have been loyal to me for years.
- I've held my basketball camps in the city for over 27 years.
- I do a lot of work in the community, both in business and for charities, and have forged solid relationships throughout the area.

All those points became part of my negotiations with the team. As a result, in addition to coaching, I was also made the vice president of business development for the team. This means that I help with marketing, ticket sales, branding, public appearances, giving speeches, building awareness of our team—important things we need to do to be a successful business entity, before I ever call my first play.

Make sure you're prepared to show your boss or potential employer the benefits that you bring. Find out what other people are earning and then go in with specifics. "I raised X dollars." "I put in 63 hours a week." "I should be earning $25,000 more than I do now because that's the market rate." If you don't ask, you'll continue to get your 2.2 percent raise every year. And if you don't ask, you have a bigger problem than the money.

If you have to back down on the money issue—and certain circumstances may require you to do so, if you want to stay with a certain company—then reevaluate your options. Take a different tack. Maybe ask for a new title. Maybe request to sit in on certain meetings. Maybe you want a new office. Maybe you want more accountability or a percentage of what you bring in. You're going to have to be flexible, and change your normal business behavior to enhance your success, as well as that of your company.

Asking for advice is an excellent strategy. When team owner Donnie Nelson initially approached me about the NBA D-League job, the first person I called was Phoenix Suns Coach Alvin Gentry to find out what he thought about it. When I was considering coming out of retirement at age 50 to play for the Detroit Shock, I called Martina Navratilova and Kevin Costner and asked them what they thought. Martina operates on pure passion, and her immediate advice was encouraging, "If anyone can do it, *you* can." Kevin, on the other hand, is a thinker. He really analyzes things, and he has my back. Kevin understands the heat. When his movie *Waterworld* came out to horrible reviews, he said that it was one of his most creative works. For him, it wasn't about what the critics said, because he was already his own toughest critic. Kevin is also an athlete; he went to Cal State–Fullerton, where he played baseball. So he knows how to win and knows how to prepare.

There were two women's professional basketball leagues in 1996. The American Basketball League (ABL) offered me close to six figures to come play for them; the WNBA offered me less. I would be 38 or 39 by the time I would play. I was sitting in my office in Omaha, Nebraska, considering both offers. That's when I called Kevin, and he said, "Nancy, I know you're going to have an opportunity to play either way, but the ABL is going to fold at some point. They're not going to make it. The WNBA is going to be here forever. In college you played in the AIAW [Association for Intercollegiate Athletics for Women conference], and it got taken over by the NCAA, so all of your AIAW records became irrelevant because of the NCAA. Don't let that happen to you twice. Go to a blue chip. Take less money and be a part of history that will last."

Kevin was right. I took $40,000 instead of $100,000, and the WNBA is going into its fourteenth year as this book is written. The ABL folded in year three.

Ladies, Dry Your Tears!

I was recently watching the Academy Awards, and I noticed something: When the women got an award, they started crying. The men, on the other hand, did not. In most cases in women's basketball—whether the team wins or loses—you'll see some players on the bench crying. Likewise, in offices, I have seen more meltdowns with women than you can imagine. The tears! I know business is tough and emotions can run high, but women have to figure out how to control them. I have a friend who was a CEO, and she would tell me how many times she would sit in her office and cry. She was stressed, she was scared, and sometimes she lost control; so she shut the door to her office and cried.

You have to be careful with that. When you lose control, you hit rock bottom emotionally. You are fragile, and that can snowball on you. Be aware that others may perceive it as weakness, and treat it as an opportunity to knock you off of the mountain you've been climbing so long and hard to stand on top of. You simply can't allow that to happen. Whatever your solution, whatever your path, you have to be able to remain in control of your feelings and how you express them. If you're in a position of leadership, or want to be, you can't make decisions based on emotion. Warren Buffett told me this: "Never make major decisions based on emotion, because you need to be thinking clearly."

I've had lots of guys tell me that they don't know how to deal with women in an emotional state in a business situation. It makes them uncomfortable; they don't know how to react. In a private setting, they might give you a hug, but in the workplace, it causes confusion and makes others ill at ease. Men often feel that women cry to manipulate them. I think you have to become self-aware and figure out how to deal with your emotions in a way that's appropriate to the situation.

Some people cry at sappy commercials; others cry at sad movies. That's okay, but crying in the office (on a regular basis) is not good. I personally try to compartmentalize my personal reactions. I don't cry after every loss. I move on, and analyze what went wrong. I look for the solutions. When I need to, I step away and gather my thoughts and myself. That's reflection, and it's useful.

When you're in a position of leadership, I admit, it can be exhausting to masquerade as one of the crowd. You're expected to lead people. But if you're at your wit's end and don't know what to do, and respond by crying and wringing your hands, who is going respect you? You *have* to manage your emotions, and show some strength and resolve. If I cried and threw the phone every time something got screwed up, I wouldn't be creating a suitable work environment. Face it: upsetting things are going to happen. You are going to "lose it" on occasion. We all do. But you have to find some sort of technique to control your anxiety and your anger. Everyone has his or her own approach. Personally, I walk away and try to compose myself. There are times when I just need some alone time to figure out what is overwhelming me at the moment. Am I scared? Maybe. Am I creating a problem that's not really there? Perhaps. Nevertheless, I have to at least *attempt* to fix it. If you can't find solutions, then you have a bigger problem, because you won't be able to move on.

If nothing else works for me, I think of Derek Jeter. He's my favorite baseball player today, as well as one of the all-time great Yankees. Doing this helps me get out of my own head, so to speak. It takes me out of where I am to a different space, and I transition my feelings. I think about his success, and his amazing calm confidence and self-awareness. I think about Derek. Try it yourself when something is bothering you: Who inspires you? Is there someone or someplace you can think of that will serve as a calming influence during frustrating times? Decide what will do this for you, and use it the next time your emotions are about to get the better of you.

 **Plays to Remember**

- *Love*. If you love what you do, you will flow with passion, energy, and enthusiasm. Success will follow.

- *Give more than you take*. This is a great rule for all aspects of life. We can all be the man in the mirror.

- *Control your emotions*. Otherwise, they can be a trap.

4

Never Fear
Success

> *Courage is knowing what not to fear.*
>
> —PLATO

Casey Coffman is the executive vice president of business development and operations for Madison Square Garden Sports, and formerly chief operating officer of Hicks Sports Group, which sold its ownership of the Texas Rangers baseball team in 2010. It still owns the Dallas Stars hockey team and half of the Liverpool Football Club (soccer), among other sports concerns, as well as entertainment and real estate holdings. As one of the few top female executives in sports, I have tremendous respect and admiration for Casey. She has always worked in male-dominated arenas, starting her career as an attorney with Coca-Cola in Asia. I remember asking her years ago how she got involved in this business, and to my surprise, she said it was because of *me*. She had heard me make a speech back in the 1980s about the importance of women being involved in sports. She figured if she couldn't play, she could make an impact on the business side. And she certainly has!

Casey faced her fears of success in what is, to this day, still a male-dominated world. She created a game plan—her own *Playbook for Success*, if you will—of how she would work her way up the ladder to get to where she is today. She used many of the same plays I am teaching you throughout this book, including dedication, concentration, goal-setting, communication, and understanding the bigger picture. But the focus of this chapter is that first step she took: facing her fears.

While it's vital that you learn to visualize your success, you won't get anywhere if you're afraid of failing. Fear acts like a blackout curtain thrown over the light of your dreams. I know for a fact that I never would have escaped the asphalt courts I played on as a scrawny teenager growing up in New York if I had been afraid of the boys whose games I infiltrated. Nor would I have been able to play in a men's professional basketball league for two years if I'd let the naysayers and substantial odds against me frighten me.

Guess what? That proposal you worked so hard on for the new business venture, the one you're sure will land you a promotion, won't do you any good as long as it remains stored as a file on your computer because you're too scared to take the next step, the one that requires you to ask your boss for a slot on the agenda at the next senior management meeting. *You can't win if you don't try.* And you can't try if fear keeps you locked in your comfort zone.

Here's a tip: The fear never goes away. In fact, the higher up the success ladder you go, the farther you have to fall, and the greater the fear becomes. The key isn't pretending that you *aren't* scared; it's learning to identify the fear and develop a game plan to overcome it—exactly what I teach here. Fear is only not knowing and controlling what we do. If you can overcome equating fear to failure, your future will be bright.

One of the most common fears is the one I just mentioned—fear of failure. We don't try because we're afraid we won't do it right; we'll be embarrassed, or someone will yell at us, or everyone will laugh at us—or all these things will happen!

Talk to Me

In general, men are really good at saying what they mean—man-to-man, face-to-face. Women, on the other hand, have a fear of face-to-face encounters and a greater tendency to talk to others about what they think about someone else. This divides the team, impedes progress and productivity, and completely disrupts the chemistry in the locker room or the office. It forces those around you to take sides, and involves people in matters in which they don't need to be involved. In short, it saps the synergy that once existed.

When I was 27, I was playing in the United States Basketball League for the Springfield Fame, in a men's league. We were down in Florida on a grueling road trip, and two guys—Andre Patterson and Ron Spivey—were jawing at each other the entire practice. Whatever the problems between them, they had been building for weeks. The two got physical in practice every day, and the tension escalated until one day Andre hit Ron on the chin, and he went down. I was standing there with my mouth open. A teammate of mine, Michael Adams, came up and told me not to worry about it. "They'll be fine," he said. "Watch, later on, they'll go get a beer together." I was thinking, *A beer? He just knocked him down, Michael. This is going to ruin our team*! But true to Michael's words, Andre and Ron had gotten whatever was bothering them out of their systems, and we moved on as a team.

Now two women who are at odds? We wouldn't do that. We're sneaky. We'd think, "divide and conquer," and end up tearing the team apart. After something like that, we could go five years without talking to each other! Don't get me wrong: I'm not saying that women should go out and clock one another to settle their disputes; rather, we must learn that we have a problem with another woman we have to talk to *her* about it—not to anyone—or everyone—else. After the other woman tells you what she thinks about you, you can say, "I don't think that's true, but I hear you." Then keep going. Try to find some common ground. Don't give up on each other too soon. You don't have to be best friends, but you can still find common ground, from which you can work, grow, and be successful together.

Women are still reaching for acceptance, and that's not always fair. That generates a lot of turmoil and distrust because they're always jockeying for that job or that position, because the plum jobs have not been in abundance or have gone to men. Some of the best advice I ever got in business is that women should never come off as angry. Okay, maybe women shouldn't show their anger, but they must learn to ask for what is fair—fair treatment, fair salary, and fair opportunity. If we could overcome this fear of trusting one another, what we'd have would be a powerful tool, known as *collaboration*.

Building trust and putting faith into relationships is a winner. It's how you treat people that makes the difference. In sports, there's always a winner and a loser. In business, both sides can share a piece of the win. That can happen individually and as a team. If we can value our partnerships with women, women empowering women, we'd all reap a huge return.

Another thing: You have to learn how to take the heat and grow from your mistakes. Don't point fingers at others. Once, during a celebrity game in Phoenix, I threw the ball out of bounds over my teammate TV star Frankie Muniz's head. He was where he was supposed to be, but I threw the ball too high. Afterward, when we were running down the court, I said jokingly, "Hey, Frankie, why didn't you jump?" Then, as I patted him on the shoulder, I followed up with, "I'll get it to you next time." Sure enough, the next time I delivered the ball to Frankie in the corner where he was supposed to be, and he hit the three. I overcame my mistake and set him up for success, because that's what good teammates do. (Hopefully, he'll give me a cameo in his next sitcom for all my good work!)

Utilize Criticism to Get Tougher and Better

Don't be afraid of sprinkling a bit of humor or dishing out light-hearted sarcasm when you're giving, or receiving, constructive criticism. It's all about learning and getting better. Criticism is going to be all around you. I'm a knowledgeable professional when it comes to television broadcasting, but I still read message boards where fans write that they hate the way I call a game. Does it sting? Yeah. Nobody likes to hear negative things like that. But I try to remember that opinions are subjective, and that I have to take the good comments with the negative ones. Everyone has an opinion, and they're entitled to voice it! Even the most talented actors, business leaders, economists, and CEOs have people somewhere who don't like them. Not everybody is going to agree with what you have to say or how you deliver your message; facing that fact is all part of taking the next step.

You *can* try to improve; you can't, however, live your life or work your job based on whether people like or dislike you. You have to do what you believe to be the right thing. You'll be confronted with both detractors and fans. I love when I hear people say, "Ah, Bernanke, what does he know?" He plays a big part in our economic picture, so he must be doing something right. They don't just hand out those jobs to people with no knowledge or experience. Likewise, I hear people say, "I hate the way Kobe Bryant plays." Everyone has an opinion of who they like and don't like. Author Stephen King isn't universally liked. Does that mean he's not a great writer? No. People have different preferences. You can't sweat that stuff.

When I sign autographs—and I sign thousands a year—I write the following phrase probably 90 percent of the time: "Never stop working, wanting, or dreaming." I fully believe in that statement. I believe that you should respect everyone and fear no one. Too often, people get so mired in fear and self-doubt that they become paralyzed and can't ascend at all, much less to the top. Facing your fears means putting yourself out there. Don't waste time focusing on your fear of failure or the judgment of others, worrying that you're not prepared or that you can't do it. The reality is that you *can. You can do it.* You have to take ownership of this attitude. If you put in the work and the hours of preparation—if you do the things you have to do—you should be confident in yourself. I guarantee, your work will flourish as a result of making that attitude adjustment.

I lived through my share of situations fraught with obstacles I had to overcome. I was too young and too inexperienced to be on the Olympic team in 1976. I've heard it all: too white, too young, too old, too slow; a girl. Talk about major problems! I've faced all of them. My life could have been one long, long list of things I "couldn't" do. But the one thing I had going for me is that *I believed I could,* and that always overrides what other people think.

You can take the same approach. My supposed shortcomings helped me. People's lack of faith in me motivated me. I like to take someone's "no" and attach it to my "yes." If you really want me to do something, don't tell me that I'm great, or amazing; tell me that you don't think I can do it, because that sets off my internal trigger. I want to show those who doubt me that they're *wrong!* I guess I like being the underdog; I get a thrill out of climbing the mountain. I like to identify who's really, really good and then figure out how I can be better.

I made the 1976 Olympic team as a high school senior because of one main reason: I identified Ann Meyers as the best player on the court. Every drill, every scrimmage, every time we had the opportunity to match up on the court, I was standing right in front of her. I wanted to guard her and to play against her. I thought that if Ann got by me, it meant that she was better than me. After all, she was the team's star; she was better than *anyone.* But if I stopped her or slowed her down, the Olympic committee would notice me and ask, "Who *is* that kid?"

I set as my challenge to dog Ann. My goal was to breathe the same air she was breathing; eventually, it paid off. There were times that I did stop Ann, and it got me noticed by the committee. I still believe today it was one of the reasons I was selected to be on the team. I didn't choose to guard someone I knew I was already better than; I chose the best player, and put it all on the line. I hadn't formulated this incredible business strategy at 17, but I did know one thing: I couldn't be afraid to compete and play against the best.

The lesson here is to always try to be more than "just as good." You should want to be better than everyone! I still seek out people who are the best; I try to surround myself with those who are smarter than I am. If I'm the smartest one, I'm in trouble. My whole team is in trouble. I want to be around brilliance. I want people to challenge me and force me to elevate my game.

As I prepare to coach my men's basketball team, I am still reaching out to my mentors—coaches, general managers, front office personnel, and officials currently in the NBA. I want to find out how they deal with the players and what they encounter in their positions. I can't get enough information. My goal is to prepare myself on all levels. When I'm not sure about something—*anything*—I pick up the phone. If it's about business, I call Warren Buffett. If it's about parenting, I call my childhood friend Barbara Wood. If it's about basketball, I call Larry Brown, Del Harris, Bob Hill, and others. I'm not afraid to ask for help. I think you gain more respect by asking and learning.

I have asked NBA MVP LeBron James of the Miami Heat about his friendship with Warren Buffett, and he says, "He's brilliant! Look at everything he's done and how he's helped so many people." I've asked Warren Buffett about LeBron, and I get a similar answer: "He's taught me more than I ever knew about being competitive." LeBron admires Warren, and Warren admires LeBron; it doesn't get any better than that. You might not think these two would have much in common, but they do. These two men, seemingly worlds apart, aren't afraid to reach out to one another for advice or help.

Fear is real, of course, but it can be overcome, if you make the effort. Fear isn't synonymous with failure, as far as I'm concerned. It represents something that's solvable. There isn't a person alive who doesn't worry about something at some point—ballplayers are afraid of being traded; executives are afraid of being fired or passed over for a promotion. Sometimes that happens, and when it does, it can be a letdown. My advice is, look for the opportunity in it. Don't dwell on the fact that someone doesn't need you or want you. Why would you want to stay where you aren't wanted, anyway? Instead, *believe* that someone else *will* want you and need you. Go find out who, and where, they are.

Learn about Overcoming
Fear from The Great Lou Holtz

Fear is a battle of the mind. If you don't win that battle, eventually you'll suck the life out of yourself and others. No doubt about it, one of the most powerful competitors you'll ever come up against is your own mind. I have seen players in sports, people in general life and business battle their own minds in an attempt to be successful and not afraid to try. So much of success is the mind-set you have. I've seen it in the locker room, on the court, and in business settings. Fear can completely derail you; literally, make you fall. I've heard Lou Holtz, the great college football coach and TV analyst tell the following story many times about overcoming fear and accepting challenges:

If I took a piece of plywood—maybe about three feet long and two feet wide—put it up on two blocks of cement a foot off the ground, and said to you, 'I'm going to blindfold you and ask you to walk across the plywood,' would you do it? If it's only a foot off the ground, what's going to happen? Your first thought would and should be a positive one of success: 'I can do that!' After all, it's not that high. You would just walk across it and think, 'That's pretty easy.'

Now, what would you say if I told you I'm going to take that same piece of wood and blindfold, and the only difference is how high I place the wood? This time, I'm going to put it between two buildings that are 50 stories high. Remember, it's the same piece of wood and the same blindfold. Will you walk across that? Now your first thought would probably be of failure, wouldn't it? The only difference is how high that wood is placed.

Here's the rub: When something *looks* easy and there's not much perceived risk, we think we can succeed. But when we set our goals high, we get scared and lose sight of success. Instead we focus on failure, the what-ifs. It's all mental.

You must not be afraid of success. It's really a cool thing to set your goals high and achieve them, but you can only do that if you let go of fear. You can do *anything* if you believe in yourself. Try not to give into fear and lose sight of success. Embrace success—don't run from it! It's one of the best feelings in the world to set a goal and achieve it. The more moments you have like that, the easier it will be for you to let go of fear in the future.

In the hit 2009 movie *The Blind Side*, football player Michael Oher, the hero and eventual Baltimore Ravens starter, had to write a high school essay on the Alfred Lord Tennyson poem "The Charge of the Light Brigade." In the poem, more than 600 light cavalry attacked a heavily fortified and defended military position. It was an impossible situation that meant certain death for many. Oher chose to describe how the poem was an illustration of courage and honor and he asked, "Should you always do what others tell you to do?" Oher concluded that any fool can have courage and that honor is the real reason you either do something or you don't.

That's so true. It's not enough to be free of fear. Shouldn't we also aim for honor and courage? And shouldn't we hope the people leading us have it, too, so they are better able to point us in the right direction to be successful?

 **Plays to Remember**

- *Never fear success.* Let go of fear and allow success to help you flourish.

- *Talk to me.* Communicate with one another, in good and bad times.

- *Utilize criticism to get tougher.* Criticism can make you better. Don't let it derail you or make you negative. Listen hard to what people are saying and make yourself better.

5

Think Like a Champion

If you want to be a champion, you've got to feel like one, you've got to act like one, and you've got to look like one.

—RED AUERBACH, LEGENDARY BOSTON CELTICS PRESIDENT

The only difference between a good day and a bad day is your attitude, beliefs, and mind-set. Whenever I think things can't get any worse, I remember the first words President Ronald Reagan spoke to his wife, Nancy, after he was shot. There he was, about to go into surgery to have the bullet of a would-be assassin removed and what does he say? "Sorry honey, I forgot to duck." That sense of humor, that ability to see past the negative is *critical* if you're going to be successful in this play. Your attitude is an absolutely vital tool.

What do I mean when I say that your attitude is a tool? Let me answer that by telling you a story.

After I started to train tennis legend Martina Navratilova back in the early 1980s, she became the number-one ranked women's tennis player in the world. Still, a lot of people kept saying that she could play well only on fast surfaces—indoors on carpet, and outdoors on grass and hard courts. In particular, the naysayers were claiming that Martina would never be able to win the French Open because it was played on the slower surface of red clay.

Her doubters were everywhere—the media and fans alike. Even Navratilova's archrival Chris Evert was quoted as saying, "Martina is a serve-and-volley player." On clay, big servers and serve-and-volley players like Martina typically don't have the advantage; the red clay slows down the game so much that it allows less athletic players to get to the ball and extend points. Martina had been hearing for so long that she couldn't win on clay that she had started to believe it herself.

Not me, though. I *knew* Martina could win the French Open. But I also knew that unless she believed it herself, it would remain an obstacle for her. Finally, I knew that she had to change her attitude and realize that she already possessed the tools and the talent she needed to be successful on *all* surfaces. If not, she would never win this coveted tournament. It was her mind-set she needed to change, and to do that we had to create a game plan for her. *If she couldn't see it, she couldn't be it.*

We started by intensifying Martina's training schedule so that she could get into better shape, enabling her to endure longer points; then we developed a strategy, or "play," for beating the traditional baseliners who traditionally dominate slow, red clay events such as the prestigious French Open. Third, we added additional shots and angles to her repertoire. More important than all the rest, though, was that she had to learn *not* to allow others to define who she was and what she could be.

I'm sure you know the end of this story: Martina accomplished what she set out to do because of an attitude adjustment. Instead of worrying about her opponents' skills, she focused on improving her own and became a more well-rounded player.

Another great example of attitude adjustment comes from Miami Dolphins quarterback Chad Pennington. In August of 2008, the New York Jets released him, in favor of signing former Green Bay Packers quarterback Brett Favre. Where did Chad wind up? With the Miami Dolphins, then one of the worst teams in the league. Chad could have sulked, and he could have whined. He could have bemoaned his fate at being cut from his old team and signed by a losing team. But did he? No.

Instead, he led the Dolphins, a team that had won only *one game* the previous year, to the American Football Conference (AFC) East division title and the Super Bowl playoffs. He set a new team record for most passes completed in a single season, and a personal-season-best for passing yards. Little wonder he was voted Associated Press Comeback Player of the Year for 2008.

Chad was able to accomplish all of that because of his approach to the season. He focused on what he *had* to do, not what others said he couldn't do. By remaining positive and confident in himself, he silenced the doubters. Sounds like Martina's story, right?

You, too, can develop an attitude like Martina's or Chad's. Sure, they have immense talent, but attitude is not about physical gifts. We can all control our attitude—and change it when we need and want to reach higher. This is critical if you are to achieve success in the workplace. For instance, let's say you have a domineering, micromanaging boss who refuses to delegate responsibility. Are you going to just give in and accept the way things are, and maybe occasionally moan about how tough it is to work for this guy? Or are you going to find ways around him, ways to be successful *in spite of him?* You can't, of course, control your boss, but you *can* control the way you react to and deal with him.

As a woman in business, you must understand the crucial importance of attitude and inner belief. Learn how to develop a positive, can-do outlook—regardless of what happens in the office. A good piece of advice is to simply stop listening to the negative people around you. We all have choices, so feel free to exercise yours in this case and ignore the negative information that drains you.

Be Determined

I was at the 1996 Olympics in Atlanta watching the women's basketball tournament with a friend of mine, Magic Johnson. (He's Magic; I'm Lady Magic. I like the name. I mean, really, who wouldn't? It works for me!) We're just sitting there watching the games, and at one point Magic looks at me and asks, "Hey Nancy, are you going to play in the WNBA next year?" (The WNBA was set to launch in 1997.)

"I don't know," I answered. "I mean, I want to, but, I'm going to be 38 when the league starts."

"Nancy Lieberman, I have never heard you say you can't do something," Magic retorted. "Do you want to play?"

"Yes."

"Then I suggest you get home and start training!," he said.

"I know," I answered somewhat sheepishly. "I've been playing in front of the janitor at the YMCA in Dallas for 17 years!"

When I returned home from Atlanta, I was *very* excited. I arrived at my house in Dallas and called for my son TJ, who was three at the time, and told him, "TJ, come in the kitchen, right now." Then I said, "TJ, answer this question for me. What does your mommy do for a living?"

"You're my mommy," he said.

"No, son, your mother is a basketball player."

"Yes, my mom's a basketball player," he repeated.

"Now, you go in there right now and you get your father and tell him that your mother is coming out of retirement. She's going to play in the WNBA."

TJ ran in the other room where my husband, Tim, was and told him, "Daddy, you're in trouble. Mommy's coming out of retirement."

Right after, TJ and Tim came walking hand-in-hand back into the kitchen, and TJ asked, "Dad, what's retirement?"

Tim didn't respond to TJ. Instead he look at me and shouted, "Nancy, are you crazy? You just got inducted last year into the Basketball Hall of Fame. What happens if you're not as good as you were? What happens if you don't hit the expectation level that people remember?"

The first thought that popped into my mind was, "Oh, my gosh: I have married Alberta Cox, the USA National Team coach who thought I was too young to play in 1976." But I didn't say that. Instead I said, "Tim, I could use a little support here! What happens if I'm better? What happens if I *surpass* expectations?"

That's the thing: You have to have it in your *heart*. You have to have it in your *soul* to be what you're going to be. It's all about *your attitude*—not what others think about you. In terms of my comeback, I was in control of my preparation, my desire, effort, organization, and game plan.

This is how it happened: I spent time in the weight room, running hills, sprinting football fields, doing agility work to increase my foot speed, and playing pickup games with the guys four days a week. I hired a former USBL teammate, Ron Spivey, to put me through grueling basketball workouts one hour a day as I prepared to take the court against players almost 20 years younger than I was.

On June 18, 1997, in Phoenix, at the America West stadium, in front of 17,000 screaming fans, I ran out onto the court wearing my number, 10, with "Lieberman" spelled out on the back. Gladys Knight sang the national anthem. The game was broadcast on NBC. Ann Meyers, my former Olympic teammate and Hall of Famer, was doing the television commentary. My coach was Cheryl Miller, another Hall of Famer and a buddy of mine. As I was standing there listening to the national anthem, overcome by a lot of emotion, that's when the reality of my hard work and preparation, putting my heart and soul into coming back, hit me: I had waited 17 years for this to happen for me. It meant so much.

People had told me: "You're too old, you're too slow, you're too this, you're too that." But there I was, 38 years old, standing there, getting ready to play. These moments mean everything in the big picture of challenging yourself and always trying to be the best you can be. When I was younger, I was a superstar. When I got older, I was a role-player.

In fact, we're all role-players at some point in our lives. At that unbelievable, poignant moment in my own life, I was thinking, "They told me I was too young in '76, and too old in '97. I mean, somebody give me something positive to hang on!" Yet I refused to believe them—both times. And both times, it got me somewhere phenomenal.

On that fabulous night in June, as I get into the game, and we're running down the court (it was *so loud* in that arena), I see my little boy in the stands, wearing a number 10 Lieberman jersey, accented with headband and wristbands. (Ironically, I had jammed my finger the day before, and I when saw my son before the game, I noticed that he had jammed his finger, too. Isn't that amazing? And he was getting his finger taped, just like mine was.) So, there's my little guy, all dressed like Mommy, right down to the finger tape, and we're running past him down the court. All of these people are yelling, and I hear this little voice shout, "Timsy" [our guard], "pass the ball to my mommy!" I'm thinking, *smart kid*!

I looked at my Australian guard and I said, "Pass the ball to the kid's mother." She did and I caught it, shot, and made my first point as a WNBA player. I hear my little boy was yelling and screaming, and you know what? I knew that all my hard work, all the hours on the court and the lifting of weights, were all for a reason.

You, too, have to find motivation for your desire to attain excellence. Think about it, there's a reason you're reading this book: You want to be better. Working hard earns you the right to be better. You have to expect success to find it. Many people will doubt you, but you can't live your life giving credence to their lack of faith. Instead, ask yourself, "What could happen if I *do* make it?" If you prepare properly, you will set yourself up for good things to happen for you. Do you have a great resume? Do you network? Are you ready for the next step and the next moment?

How you deal with your customers or coworkers is all about attitude. A smile and some warmth go a long way. When I walk into a room to meet someone I know, I give that person a hug and say, "Hi, how are you? How's it going?" The way we communicate each day, the attitude we put forth, is going to affect how *we* affect the lives of others. You know how good it feels when somebody puts a hand on your shoulder, remembers your name, or pats you on the back to indicate "job well done." I always try to be warm and friendly. Being cold and disconnected gets you nowhere! A sincere handshake, a pat on the back or shoulder, or a hug—if you happen to know the person well enough and it feels comfortable— all work wonders.

As I said earlier, I use a lot of humor in my interactions with others; I do so because I think humor is an important tool. I mean, don't people like to laugh? I *love* to laugh. I laugh with, and at, Charles Barkley whenever I see him. It's usually something like, "Charles, have you hurt anybody on the golf course lately?" Or, "Charles, people are saying that the reason Tiger lost that golf event is because he's watching you swing your club, and it's screwing up his golf swing." Have fun with people!

Humor can also be a great equalizer among people who appear "unequal." I use humor with everyone, *especially* the people for whom I have great respect, like Warren Buffett. "Warren," I'll say, "If Bill [Gates] isn't going to use all those billions you gave him, I could use some, okay? I have a kid. Kid needs to eat." He just laughs at me, either because he thinks I'm crazy or because he enjoys it when somebody makes him laugh. Laughter is relaxing. It's a wonderful tool that you can use *every single day*.

Confidence and trust—those are two other characteristics you communicate through your attitude *every single day*. You interact with countless people—your families and friends, your employees and managers, and strangers. I'm not saying it's going to be a smooth ride all the way; clearly, there are going to hurdles along the way. Again, it's how we handle the difficult situations that will determine whether we become successful or not.

I repeat: Don't let anybody tell you what you can't be. I say this often throughout the book because it's so important. Keep telling people—your managers, your associates, your downline, and your customers—what you *can* be. Your attitude and belief are contagious; those around you will notice and appreciate your mind-set. To me, trust means that you believe that you—and others—are making solid choices that will help you get closer to your desired goal. If *you* don't trust and believe in yourself, why should others? It's difficult—nearly impossible—to make a relationship work without trust. When doubt creeps in, you will almost always end up second-guessing yourself and others. You have to provide a reason to pull together, to turn any situation into a success story.

You Are Who You Think You Are

When I got the coaching job with the Detroit Shock, we were an "expansion team," which meant that we were brand new to the league. As such, we were predicted to take last place in the WNBA that year. That was okay with me, though. As far as I was concerned, I didn't care what people thought about us. The only thing that mattered was what *we* thought about each other.

And wouldn't you know it? We went 17 and 13 that first season, missing the playoffs by a mere half game. We had the best expansion record in the *history of sports*, all because we believed in ourselves and in each other. Our success came about because of our positive attitude and abiding trust in one another. Our goal was for each player to focus daily on making individual improvements, which each of them did. As a result, we proved to be a formidable team, from the opening buzzer.

If you do well by yourself, that's fantastic. But a woman alone can more easily be broken. Give me one number two pencil, and I can snap it in half with no trouble. Give me 15 pencils bound together with even a thin rubber band and they become unbreakable. Together as a team, with the right attitude, you're too strong to beat. Even on your worst day, set your standards higher than your competitors on their best day. That's mental attitude.

I've played for 29 coaches in my basketball career, and each of them had a different leadership style. The most demanding coach I ever played for was the University of Tennessee's Pat Summitt. She required *everything* of me. She never allowed me to be satisfied with where I was. She was always encouraging me to go to places I didn't even think I could go, which gave me a sense of mental strength that subsequently pushed me physically, as well. Looking back, I can see that her influence definitely paid off for me. She motivated me beyond any sense of doubt, and took me to a mental level that I didn't know existed. I will never again be afraid to go beyond what I consider my "comfort zone."

When I was in college—and I say this humbly—I was better than my teammates. The one thing that I thought about every day in practice was that I was *not* going to play down to their level; they were going to have to come up to meet *mine*! That's attitude. My job, every day, was to try and raise them up to my level of play. I didn't do this by insulting them or telling them that they were terrible; I just tried, through my actions, to show them the bigger picture of what success could be: *If we do this, we can win. If we do this, we can be the best team that ever played college basketball.*

When you are better or more talented at something than others, you have two options: You can either demean and defeat them, or you can bring them along with you to the top. I wanted to empower my teammates to be the best. We all have that capability, every day, to be better. A lot of being better requires having the right attitude and confidence—real confidence, not the fake kind.

You can have fun with your attitude, yet remain humble. I've accomplished a lot in my life, but at 51 I am *far* from finished. The next level for me would be to own a pro sports team one day, coach in the NBA, or work for a Fortune 500 company. I'm friends with many successful men: Warren Buffett, Roger Staubach, Tony Dorsett, Charles Barkley, Muhammad Ali, Jerry Colangelo, Donald Trump, Michael Jordan, Magic Johnson, and numerous others. It's really kind of cool. I have a great life. I'm a woman who interacts every day in business and sports. I find that people respond to me because I generally care, love sports, and talk the talk. I'm *real*; and I love to hear and share stories of success. Life's Golden Rule is all about attitude. It's a simple concept. If you're warm and engaging, wouldn't you rather do business with people you like? I mean, how does it make you feel when somebody is cold, and shows you through his or her body language? I believe that if you are comfortable around people, it's easier to read them. Look them in the eyes.

What do you connect on? Sports, arts, history? Find *something*. It's bound to be there.

One of the highlights of my career—besides being inducted into the Basketball Hall of Fame in 1996—was playing for my country as a kid in the Olympics. Viewers who tune in to the Olympics might not know the athletes personally, but they're always pulling for them. For their part, the athletes are playing to hear that anthem and see the flag go up. I still get chills just thinking about it. It's a wonderful bond that forms among the athletes. It's about attitude and faith, and playing for something bigger than yourself.

I was a role-player in the '76 Olympics. I wasn't necessarily a star, but because I was so young, I brought a lot of energy and enthusiasm to the team. I was a piece of the puzzle, an important one. You can be really good when you work with others to achieve a greater goal. My job at that time was simply to be ready when the moment presented itself. There was no drama. I pushed my teammates to challenge and improve themselves each day in practice. You, too, can be a positive force as a role-player in any business situation.

When my son, TJ, was just a little guy in elementary school, I went to talk to his teacher on parent/teacher conference day. The principal at Jackson Elementary School saw me and said, "Ms. Lieberman, we were so excited about you coming to speak."

I said, "What?"

"Yes," he continued, "TJ has scheduled you to speak to the school in April."

"Really?" I said. "I would be delighted."

"TJ said you would bring your silver medal from the Olympics, and autograph posters for the students," he added. "You'll be speaking for 45 minutes, and then we'll have 15 minutes of Q&A."

I said, "Okay—and TJ set this up for me, correct?"

Later, I told TJ, fine, I would do this, but he would have to introduce me at the assembly; more, I put him in charge of my Olympic medal. I set some rules for my medal—especially for the kids. They weren't allowed to chew on it, steal it, or slam it against the wall. TJ actually had to take care of it.

All the students in the school were given an opportunity to wear the medal and hold it, to give them a little sense of that attitude I'm describing here. It reminded me how lucky I was to be a part of that team. It gave me some of the attitude and swagger that I still count on today. I learned teamwork and tasted success. Being a part of the Olympics was bigger than any one person individually. And years later, every one of my son's classmates who got a chance to wear that medal could feel it, too.

My First Meeting with the Champ

Prior to my senior year at Old Dominion, I was asked to appear at the New York Stock Exchange in New York City (no, not to ring the bell, it was for the Olympic Committee). I then found out that my hero, Muhammad Ali, was going to be there, too. I couldn't believe they were having us do it together. I could hardly breathe because he was so close.

My best friend growing up, a woman named Barbara Wood, and my mother, Renee, accompanied me. It was my mother's assignment to talk to Ali. She began, "Mr. Muhammad, hi, how are you?" He just looked at her and said nothing. She continued, "My daughter, Nancy—she's over there, the redhead. My daughter's the greatest basketball player of all time." To this he replied, simply, "Lady, *I* am the greatest of all time."

Then Muhammad looked at this other man, Howard Davis, who had been on the Olympic boxing team in 1976, and said, "Howard, the lady says the kid's the greatest." Before responding, Howard looked over at me and said, "Yeah, she is the champ!"

At this point, Muhammad called me over: "Kid, come on over here. Your mom says that you're the greatest basketball player of all time." I told him, "Yeah, I'm good. I'm the best!" He hugged me then, and told me that he was proud of my honest answer. "That's excellent, Nancy. You know, most people would not say that they were good. But me, I'm the greatest of all time." And he is.

That night, Muhammad invited my mom, Barbara, and me to his hotel suite at The Plaza Hotel. We sat there for two hours while he told us about his philosophy of life and boxing. It was amazing. We even exchanged phone numbers! I was thinking, "Come on. This is ridiculous!"

Later, back at Old Dominion University, as I was heading into my senior year, *Sports Illustrated* did a 14-page story on me in the college basketball issue. Throughout the article, I was quoted describing how much I loved Muhammad Ali. Well, he read it, and called me at my college apartment. My friend Wes answered the phone, then called to me: "Nancy, some guy is on the phone saying he's the champ, Muhammad Ali."

I ran to the phone and said, "Hello?"

I heard his unmistakable voice say, "Nancy, it's Muhammad Ali."

I stammered, "Hi, how are you?"

He was so friendly and matter-of-fact. Here was the champion of the world, a man I never thought would care that much about me, taking the time to reach out to me. And ever since, he has been incredibly kind to me. He and his wife, Lonnie, have invited me to come out to their house whenever I've been in Scottsdale, Arizona, where they live. How amazing is that?

Every time I see Muhammad, I get choked up because he's so remarkable. He has taught me so much about attitude, generosity, and humility—even considering what has happened to him later in life. One of the greatest communicators of all time now faces a challenge every time he wants to interact because of his physical limitations, caused by Parkinson's disease. Yet he keeps reaching out, with humor and love. He and his wife—who has amazing grace, a great sense of humor, and a deep love for her husband— are truly an inspirational pair. Lonnie graciously shares him with all of us. Together, they have written a life chapter in selflessness and giving.

I challenge you to live your life with that kind of attitude. Every day you walk into your office, don't think, it's another nine-to-five day (or eight-to-six, as it frequently is these days). Think about how you can get better. You can experience self-improvement every single day, from the moment you wake up. You have the ability to influence people's lives with just a smile, a high five, a "nice job," or a kind word. When I play basketball and I make a nice pass to a teammate and he or she scores, you know the first thing I do? I point, slap, and give a pat on the back. I acknowledge the connection. If somebody around you does something good, tell him or her! You may often think it but then don't bother to say it because you get busy. I always encourage what I call 360-degree communication— the full circle. Even if you are the boss, you have to be willing to hear what others think. It can be a great asset for you.

The most important thing you can do is communicate with one another. I and my colleagues do that all the time. We tell our players, make sure you're talking. Every drill we run, we tell them, say the person's name that you're passing to. We want to communicate with one another as coaches and as players. The more people feel that you're interested in what they have to say, the more value and information you have and can share. In most cases, people you work with want to be heard. Being the boss is a good thing, even though it comes with a lot of responsibility and decision-making pressure. You're in a position to receive and listen to suggestions. Just remember that you're the one who has to make the final decision.

Attitude is about believing in one another, knowing how to execute, having the confidence to think outside the box, and learning to trust yourself. I don't know you, and you don't know me, but if right now we were going to play a pickup game against two opponents, I'm going to believe that we will win because I'm going to trust that you're going to make me better and set me up for success. We have never been on the basketball court together before, but if you're my teammate now, I have to believe in you. It's called blind trust, and it matters!

Selective Hearing Not Allowed

Korie Hlede of Duquesne University was my number one pick in the 1998 WNBA draft for the Detroit Shock. I remember one practice when she was absolutely on fire. I don't think she missed a shot for two and a half hours. Our coaching staff couldn't have been more complimentary to her regarding her brilliant play that day. We were like her personal cheerleaders. Toward the end of the practice, however, in one of our offensive sets, she was supposed to set a screen for her teammate, and she didn't. I let her know that Sandy was depending on her to set the screen so that she could get open and make the shot. It's an important detail in basketball when we're trying to execute, and I reminded her of that fact. That one criticism, however, completely deflated her, even though we'd been telling her for two hours how great she was. After practice, she slumped in front of her locker, clearly feeling dejected. I was astonished! We could not have been more positive throughout the practice.

I sent for one of my assistant coaches and we played "Good Coach, Bad Coach." My assistant went over to Korie, sat down, and repeated all of the good things we had said to her during practice. He then explained to her that we have to get the little things right, too, in order to make both her and our team better—to set us up for success. It didn't help. Korie walked away from that outstanding practice remembering only one thing: that Coach was mad at her for not setting a screen.

That was an important learning moment for me as a young coach. It helped me become a better manager. I learned that instead of just saying, "Korie, come on! You didn't set the screen!," I needed to do more. I needed to explain to her, in that moment, *why* it was so important. It wasn't until after my assistant coach translated for me that she understood it. I learned that day that not only did I have to explain *what* I wanted, but *why* I wanted it, as well.

The psychology of coaching people up (coaching them to another level) and balancing constructive criticism is a mental minefield, because it's about what *you* believe. If you think your coach, boss, or coworker dislikes you when you face the heat from one of them, that's what you're going to believe. But before you get too down on yourself, stop and consider the source of the criticism. Does this person have a history of beating people down? Instead of quitting, deal with his or her criticism by, first, listening to it, and then applying it. Use it as a teachable moment. In most cases, some of what we hear is usually true, though we might not like hearing it. Try your best to be objective. Evaluate unemotionally what's being said to you and try to determine whether that is truly how certain people view you. Take the information and run with it! It's only going to make you better. We really do improve the most when we experience losses or failure.

If you determine that the source or content of the criticism is fraudulent, let it go. Rumor-mongers and naysayers are at every turn, looking to tear people down. Keep your distance from them, and move on.

Be Someone's Hero

When I used to go to Harlem at night and was the only white kid playing in Rucker Park, I was nervous, but I had a no-fear attitude! The guys would look at me and wonder, "What are *you* doing here?" I would look right back at them with the same question in my eyes. I asked one of them, "Is your name Rucker? No? So, if it's not your park, then I have next." That attitude cut through a lot of barriers. It gave guys a reason to want to see if I could play; when I proved I could, it gave me the right to stay on that court, play together, and win. We formed a sense of trust, and a bond.

Haven't we all experienced this kind of thing before? Usually the only difference between a good day and a bad day is your attitude and belief. It's okay to want to be better. It's okay, if you're willing to pay the price and have some attitude, as long as its tempered with humility and a little humor, and backed by execution and trust. If you can achieve that, the sky's the limit. I will say this, however:

Don't expect what you don't give. If you are willing to work harder than the rest, take them up with your attitude. It isn't just about you. You also have to have the confidence to reach out to others and raise them to your level. Make it your goal to be someone's hero.

I want to be my son's hero, as I've said before, but not just because I am an accomplished athlete and businesswoman. You should want to be somebody's hero every day, in your home, at work, in the gym. This goal should be a consistent part of who you are. I strive to inspire people on a daily basis. I am honestly thankful for the incredible career I've had. Every moment has been amazing, from the Olympics to playing in men's and women's professional leagues and, now, to coaching in the NBA Development League. But *nothing* is more important to me than being a good mom and a good person. The world is overrun with takers. Be different, by always giving generously and with sincerity.

I have always maintained that to excel at something, you must train for it and think like a champion. It's what I have done throughout my career. You have to think, believe, and compete. If you can master this three-part strategy, you will perform consistently and, ultimately, reach your goals to win and succeed. Today's athletes apply a lot of visualization techniques; they "see" themselves succeeding. This can be applied in business, too. Remember, think positively and visualize success.

What I definitely *do* know is that to succeed in any facet of life, you have to have the mind-set of a champion, full of positive and powerful thoughts. This has been a major force for me and others in sports, and it can be for you in your career. You can train your mind to develop a positive and powerful vision of what you need to do to help you work toward your goals. Doing so will also influence how others around you work.

Sadly, it has become a bad habit for many people to speak negatively, about themselves, others, or situations that can take us down. Stop! Don't be one of them. Be strong; refuse to allow negativity to cloud or control the methods that enable you to think and act clearly. Make your mind-set your edge. If you are negative, or allow others around you to be so, it will hurt your own and your team's performance. To be a champion, you have to *see* yourself as one.

 **Plays to Remember**

- *Have the mind-set of a champion.* Your attitude and belief are key to winning.

- *Challenge yourself daily.* Decide what you want and map out your plan for success.

- *Be a hope-giver.* Encourage others to be successful, and show them how to do it.

6

It's All about Teamwork

Talent wins games, but teamwork and intelligence wins championships.
—MICHAEL JORDAN, HALL OF FAME BASKETBALL PLAYER

"Teamwork" has many definitions. Early in my career, my coaches shared the adage, "There is no 'i' in team." But as many players in business and sports have come to recognize, there *is* an "i" in win. This, my friends, can produce a delicate balance of overachievers, role-players, and a variety of different strengths that make up any team.

I am a firm believer that you have to have the talent to win; but you can't do it by yourself if the effort requires you to work with teammates. Teamwork requires the ability to recognize the talent and abilities of others and apply them to one final objective. It's tough to be ambitious and set lofty goals and hope that others around you have the same or at least a similar mind-set for succeeding together. Many companies pride themselves on hiring talent and getting them to work in a cohesive group setting, coordinating efforts as a team rather than relying upon one talented individual's effort. However, there are so few examples of this kind of teamwork in business, so sports analogies are often used to drive home how vital team building and working together are to growing a business.

What often causes problems is the attention that's typically given to a particular individual who has had enormous success. Our society is much more fascinated with individual accomplishments than the collective team's victory. This narrow focus can make a team's accomplishments seem secondary. Teamwork depends on hard work, cooperation, and the skill level of *all* the individuals on the team. You will win and lose as a team, though no doubt there will be people who become stars and deserve the spotlight.

Players *always* have a choice. They can play as a team or play like individuals. The latter option has a tendency to cause turmoil and internal discord, and can disturb the overall team's mind-set. I realized during my time playing at Old Dominion that the overall knowledge base of our team grew exponentially because we could bounce ideas off one another, discuss techniques, and increase one another's value to our collective success. Teamwork required total commitment from each member of the team. That's critical: Your success is closely linked to the success of your team.

Consider the race between Barack Obama and Hillary Clinton for the Democratic presidential nomination. Clinton's campaign team was a mess of infighting and dueling egos. After the campaign, numerous articles and books chronicled the fact that her advisors couldn't align to execute their strategy. To the end, they routinely attacked and undermined each other. Obama's campaign, in contrast, has been praised for its organization, military precision, focus, single-minded leadership, and absence of drama—thus the moniker "No drama Obama."

Could the fact that many of the top people on Clinton's staff were women have been part of the problem? Although I hate to say it, I have observed time and again that women do not always work well with other women on teams. They are at times quick to criticize and sabotage their female coworkers, and to hold back information from them. They tend to go behind each other's backs and form hurtful—and unproductive—alliances. That's why this chapter—this play—focuses on team building. Unfortunately, too many women forget, or never learned, the adage that there's no "i" in team. They get scared, and worry that the pie is still too small for all of them to get a piece; or they want a bigger piece. Often, they are insecure in regard to their positions on the team. They suspect they may be the "token woman," so they want to make sure another woman doesn't take their coveted, albeit lonely, spot.

Too often, women fail to understand the importance of sharing—be it information, skills, or support. Whereas athletes know all too well that if you don't share, you divide the team, hence reducing its effectiveness. I admit I've been guilty of this myself. I learned this lesson at a young age, while playing for Old Dominion University. During my first two years in college, I took every shot I could and was already a Kodak All-American and ranked one of the best players in the country. Then one day my coach, Hall of Famer Marianne Stanley, took me aside and asked me to pass more, to help make everyone around me better. She promised that if I did this, we would win a championship. Prior to that instruction, I had considered myself to be one of the most unselfish and kind teammates. Boy was I kidding myself.

Old Dominion was very successful. In 1977 we had just come off winning the Women's National Invitational Tournament. We went 30–4 that season. Not only were we were really good, together we had the foundation to reach a higher level, which was to win a national championship.

After my coach asked me to pass more and shoot less, it took more than a minute or two for me to accept the thought of not scoring 25 points a game. I was the point guard of the team, after all. She was asking me to make a sacrifice, and it was difficult for me to even consider at first; but I thought about it and, eventually, saw the wisdom of her plan.

When I showed up for my junior year at Old Dominion as the leader, the point guard (the associate and the manager), my job was to ask myself a single question: "Do I make *me* better, or do I make the people around me better?" I chose to make the sacrifice—reluctantly, to be quite honest. It paid off—in spades! My junior year, 1979, Old Dominion went 37–1, and we won our first national championship, by beating Louisiana Tech. My senior year, 1980, we went 35–1 and took our second national title, by beating the University of Tennessee—and my friend Pat Summitt. It also paid off for me, personally: I was two-time Player of the Year in women's college basketball. Just as important, my teammates Inge Nissen and Anne Donovan became All-Americans in those seasons, as well.

The point is, I accomplished my own individual goals while helping my team with the most important goal: to be the best. Yes, I shot about 15 fewer times a game, but I achieved my personal success in a more meaningful way. Old Dominion University went 72–2 those last two years, and we won *as a team*.

I ask you that same question right now: Do you make *you* better, or do you make your colleagues, employees, and clients better? Or do you make those around you better only on the days that you feel good about yourself? Needless to say, when you pop into the office and you've had a really good day, and you're really in a lighthearted and interactive mood, it's easier to share your energy. But what about the hard days, the days that you don't feel good and you're a little bit cranky? (I know this *never* happens to us women!) Imagine for a moment that this is your mood on a given day, and you walk into your office with that look, that attitude—you know the one I mean. People watch what you do, how you act. If you're a leader, you are being observed *every single day*. How you walk, how you talk, your attitude, your words, your appearance, the way you communicate. Especially the young people around—those in whom you've invested to grow your business—are paying close attention to you.

I know that if I walk onto the court or into the locker room with a bad attitude, apparent from my body language, choice of words, and reluctance to look people in the eyes, then I'm in trouble, and so is my team. If I don't share what I'm thinking or feeling, and instead just walk by and ignore my teammates, they are going to know it. I'm going to have a negative effect on my team.

You should strive to be the best you can every single day, whether you're having a good or bad day. As I stated previously, the only difference between these two states of mind is the attitude with which you meet them, and a willingness to admit that you *can and do* influence your team. Embracing the belief that you can be the best you can be, even on bad days, is entirely up to you. It's about accountability and responsibility—which we all have to accept in order to achieve a level of greatness.

Women *can* be part of and lead teams as well as men. We *can* learn to be unselfish and talk through problems, instead of pitting ourselves against one another. We *can* learn to surround ourselves with upbeat, successful people who make us better. To do so takes open and honest, proactive and positive communication—the most crucial component for winning as a team!

Knowing your role is another critical factor of effective teamwork. Are you a guard, designed to create plays for and energize your team? Are you a rebounder, consistent and reliable in your talent to come away with the ball, but often out of the spotlight? Or are you a floor leader, charged with interpreting the coaches' instructions and understanding the talent around you? Always remain clear about what your job is; your teammates are counting on you to get it done.

After my first season in the WNBA, I was offered a position as the head coach and general manager for the Detroit Shock. I didn't want to go in there with this expectation that, well, you know, it's Nancy, and she's supposed to be successful. I did have the advantage of calling on some great coaches who were also friends: longtime Duke men's basketball coach Mike Krzyzewski, University of Tennessee women's basketball coach Pat Summitt, Stanford University women's basketball coach Tara VanDerveer, and legendary Indiana and Texas Tech men's basketball coach Bobby Knight. Detroit Pistons head coach Doug Collins was also a reliable resource for me on a daily basis, always willing to share everything he knew about the game. I could call these pros and ask, "What do you think?" or, "How have you done this?" or, "I'm thinking about doing this; what's your opinion?" The first step toward being a member of a team is to be ready and willing to reach out to others who are sources of valuable information. The second step is to share that information, to filter it down to others.

A Promise to the Team

It was senior night in Norman, Oklahoma, 2009, and Courtney Paris, a four-time All-American, had just played her last home game for the Oklahoma University Sooners. Courtney was one of the top collegiate women's basketball players in the country. She had broken at least 20 NCAA records during her college career at Oklahoma University, including being the only player in NCAA history, male or female, to make 700 points, 500 rebounds, and 100 blocks in a season—outdistancing male superstars like Kareem Abdul-Jabbar and Oscar Robinson. She had not only set the bar higher in women's basketball but also had redefined what it meant to be consistent throughout her collegiate career.

Now she was about to do it again, this time off the court. With no prompting, she announced that if the Sooners didn't win the NCAA women's championship, she would refund her scholarship—all four years of it, valued at $64,000. It was a promise she had discussed ahead of time with her father, as a way to show her teammates, coaches, and fans how much confidence she had that her team could win it all.

When I interviewed her about it, she remained adamant that she would give the money back if they didn't go all the way. I couldn't stop asking, "Are you sure?" And she kept telling me, "I meant it. I am a woman of my word."

At the time, the Sooners were already an outstanding team, with solid confidence, but as I watched over the next couple of weeks it was clear that Courtney's pledge was taking them to a whole new level. The transformation was amazing. You could see her teammates rallying around her, determined to play harder, to support her belief in them. That's what true team spirit is about. I love that Courtney wasn't afraid to go after something that meant so much to her. How many women do you know would do a thing like that?

The Sooners did make it to the final four, and to the championship game, where they lost to Louisville 61–59. The university graciously refused to accept Courtney's offer of a tuition refund. But her unselfish nature remains unchanged: She plans to set up some kind of fund to support the needy in Oklahoma. Courtney now plays in the WNBA for the Chicago Sky, and you'd better believe her teammates there know they can count on her.

The reality is that without that kind of team spirit and commitment, you simply will not win, or even come close—on or off the court.

Teamwork Defined

Like so many other issues I've covered so far in my *Playbook for Success*, I believe that teamwork comes down to attitude. It comprises the ability to give, support, and see a picture bigger than one with just you in it. It requires that you define your goals, and understand how they mesh with those of your coworkers, your department, and the company itself.

I recall one company I visited several years ago that, in my estimation, had a very effective way of ensuring that all its employees worked toward the greater good of the entire team. The organization's senior management met for two days annually to map out, at a macro level, companywide goals for the coming year. Senior managers then passed those goals down to the middle managers, who directed the departments. They, in turn, shared these goals with their employees and developed their own departmental goals, which were designed to help meet the overall company objectives. Finally, each individual employee then develops his or her own goals designed to help the department—and, hence, the company—meet *its* goals.

Middle managers took this cooperative approach a step further. Before their departmental goals were finalized, they met and shared them to make sure all were in alignment, that none would throw up barriers or problems that might impede another department's chance of success. Only then were the goals finalized and passed up to senior management.

Oh, and one other thing: Everyone's bonuses depended not only on their ability to meet their individual goals, but on the department and the company as a whole doing so as well. The company worked like a beautifully stacked wall of fieldstone—each piece strong and effective, yet dependent on the others to succeed.

Now *that's* teamwork!

Another example of teamwork comes from my own experience as coach and general manager of the Detroit Shock. I was brand new to a company where a number of employees had worked for years. I needed to hire an executive assistant, and I wanted someone who knew the lay of the land, the politics, where the proverbial bodies were buried, and how things got done. I needed someone who would partner with me, to make me—and, thus, the team—successful. So I asked Palace Sports and Entertainment president, Tom Wilson, the man who hired me, if I could hire *his* executive assistant Judy Romero, a savvy woman who had worked in the organization for years. To Tom's credit, because he wanted what was best for the team, not just for himself, he let me sign her on as my right hand.

Building a Team

Of course, you don't build a team overnight, particularly if your current department or company has been functioning more like a reality television program than a well-oiled machine. Nevertheless, I want you to start on this project right now.

You have to begin by asking yourself tough questions:

- Who are my personnel?
- Do their strengths and weaknesses fit our team?
- What's the chemistry like?
- Are we being productive and moving toward our goals?
- Do we need to make changes and reassign people?
- How do we stack up to the competition?

These are all difficult questions you have to answer when building your team. In this way, you will eventually find common ground on which to meet, where you can find solutions to problems!

Before you make any decisions, talk to the individuals on your team. Define goals for them, as well as incremental measurements they are expected to hit along the way. Then, if they don't, ask why not. It's a simple question. Are there problems we didn't foresee? How can I help you? Conversely, when employees are doing a fantastic job, tell them that you appreciate it—let then know you noticed. Pat them on the back. Tell them in front of the group, or privately, whichever is most appropriate, that you're proud of what they've done. Appreciation goes a long way toward pulling others up to their level.

Maybe you work in the production department and you're tired of the sales manager overcommitting. Sit down and make a list of your concerns, then describe what you would like to see happen to resolve them. Make sure to include the things that *you* can do in return to help the sales manager with your requests. Then invite him or her to lunch.

Begin discussing your list at the restaurant (or in any other nonthreatening environment). Keep the conversation positive. Instead of saying, for example, "You always tell customers we can deliver in two weeks when you know we need at least a month to process those orders," try something like, "I know there's been a disconnect between what the customer expects and what we've been providing. How can we improve on that?" Spell out your challenges and *listen* to his or hers in return. By listening and sharing, you'll eventually find common ground from which to move forward!

I always wanted to be part of a team. However, in order for this to happen, I had to achieve success on an individual level. Everybody says, "Well, you know, that's basketball. It's all about teamwork." True, basketball *is* about teamwork, to a large degree; but I can help make my team better by working on myself. If you're not performing well as an individual, you're not going to be a good member of the team.

So when people say that "it's just about the team," they do have a point, because teamwork is how we make each other better. But there's also individual accountability and responsibility; we all have the ability to improve, to take ourselves to a higher level, whether it's dealing with a customer, associates, or managers. We can all be better.

The first step is to enhance communication. As a point guard, I have to be able to communicate with everyone around me—my teammates. I certainly can't say to one player, "Boy, you're bad. You're *really* bad. I won't be giving you the ball." I mean, I can't do that to my teammate. My job is to empower those around me. My job is to find out what their strengths and weaknesses are, and then find the play or the plan to make the most of the strengths and mitigate the weaknesses.

I had a teammate at Old Dominion named Angela Cotman. Even if I sent Angela a memo that said, "By the way, I will be throwing you a bounce pass in the game today," she still couldn't catch it. So why would I throw Angela a bounce pass and set her up for failure; why wouldn't I throw her the kind of pass she could catch, one that would set her up for success? I was the decision maker; I had the ball. Her success was, literally, in my hands. She and I had many conversations during the course of our four years together about how I could help make her better. It was so simple. It was as basic as asking the question: What can I do to make you better? Most of us don't ask this important question of our friends and coworkers often enough.

I've been a friend of hockey great Wayne Gretzky's since 1981, and we have talked many times, as I have with Magic Johnson and Phoenix Suns future Hall of Famer Steve Nash, about how to deliver the puck or ball to our teammates. We're all known for our ability to make passes, because we never put the ball or the puck where a player is but where he or she *should be*. I would not pass the ball to teammates when they were not in the right place. It was my job to direct them and get them the ball where they would be most affective. As a manager, you have to lead people in the same way— not to where they are, but to where they need to be.

As managers, it's absolutely critical to find out what individuals' strengths and weaknesses are. How can you make them better by enhancing their strengths? How you can encourage them to overcome their weaknesses?

When I coached in the WNBA, I had players to whom I could just say, "Hey Jennifer, you're not getting it done. You're not setting the screens. This is what I need you to do instead," and she'd be fine with it. On the other hand, if I had used that same tone with another player, it might crush her. With Rhonda, for example, I might have to ease into it: "You know what? I really need you to actually run the play right, because if you run the play right, Rhonda, I get my contract renewed." I would use a little humor, but with a definite message attached. Selfish, maybe; meanspirited, no, not really. Some people just need to understand the bigger picture. *If you do this, this is how it's going to affect our players and our team, your coworkers, and our company.*

The lesson here is that you might have to communicate with one employee or colleague differently than you would another. It's critically important to remember that each of us is different, and that we handle both criticism and even compliments differently. Business is not a democracy. Not everyone is always going to be treated equally. I know that's hard to swallow, but it's true. You know people who can't take a compliment, don't you? Your job as a leader is to disseminate information. Because of this, you need to know how each individual on your team is going to react, and you have to tailor your input on that basis. Your job is to make all of them the best they can be because, trust me, you can't be the best unless *they* are!

To be a good teammate, you have to understand all aspects of your business and game plan. There are times you will just have to be a sponge. Listen and absorb information around you and keep your mouth shut. If you surround yourself with people who know more than you do, it's okay if you happen to lack experience. Make it up with vision, instinct, and an ability to articulate what your team needs to do. Regardless of age and experience, you can always be passionate, tenacious, and determined. You can always complete the tasks that are put in front of you. I played on many a team that won through sheer willpower and the force of the individual personalities.

You can't underestimate the power of cheering others on to success, either. When I'm telecasting from the Dallas Mavericks basketball games, I can't help but smile when they show fans on the jumbo screen cheering—really, going nuts. The sight of these enthusiasts gets the crowd whipped into a frenzy in less than a minute. Cheering really does make a difference, which is why professional sports teams call the fans the sixth man in basketball, or the twelfth man in football. Similarly, there's truth to "home court advantage." You will run up against people who are not self-starters, who rely on your enthusiasm; they need to be motivated, not demoralized. That doesn't mean you can't ever offer criticism. When I watch film with players, I will point out what they did wrong, but I always end on a positive note. It's imperative to celebrate the good in people. Sometimes all it takes is a pat on the back, a point across the room, an e-mail or text message.

You have to have social skills. If you're working in an office and you ride up in the elevator with someone, ask how he or she is. Try to remember people's names. Even if you don't really care, fake it. I know the impression it leaves on me when someone remembers to ask about TJ or my mom. Simple acts of kindness like these are important to building strength and cohesiveness on your team.

I know this guy named Brad Thomas. Every year on my birthday, I get a phone call from him, even if I haven't seen him in 10 years. It's really such a cool thing. He remembers people's birthdays, and people remember him for it. That's an important part of building relationships: remembering details of people's lives, hearing what they have to say. Years ago I remember Bill Clinton saying he was going to make listening an aerobic activity. Too few of us really listen when someone else is talking. When I was coaching in Detroit, I called a time-out just to call a specific play called "horns." I diagrammed it, being careful to keep it simple. As the team ran back out on the floor, one player turned around and came back to ask me, "What are we running?" I was astonished. With this play— that I had *just spelled out*—we would win or lose the game. Yet somehow, she hadn't heard me! I walked her back onto the court and explained again, "We're running horns, and I would appreciate it if you hit the shot because this play is all about you!" She did, and we won!

Plays to Remember

- *Work as a team.* There's no greater feeling of satisfaction than playing/working as a team. When you win collectively, it will be a story that's told for years.

- *Keep your promises.* Don't make a promise if you can't deliver. It's your credibility you're highlighting.

- *Ask the key questions.* How can I make you better? What can I do for you? What do you need to succeed? When can we meet to talk about it?

7

Do Your Homework

The will to win is important, but the will to prepare is vital.
　　　　—JOE PATERNO, HALL OF FAME COLLEGE FOOTBALL COACH

Do you know what every professional sports team and player does before a game? They watch hours and hours of video of their opponents. They look at pages upon pages of statistics on themselves and those they will face on the field or the court. By game day, we know their strengths and weaknesses as well as we know our own, and we've made the necessary adjustments in our own play to take advantage of that knowledge. Preparation takes the guesswork out of what you are about to encounter.

Everyone has basic tendencies in all that they do, whether its sports or business. And one thing is true in either field: It always helps to put together a hotshot team that you trust. Game plans and strategies change in the professional world, as do personnel and business environments. We must be prepared for change, and how prepared we are will be determined by how flexible we are. It's always necessary to have a contingency plan in place.

I still laugh today when I look back at how Martina Navratilova and I changed the women's tennis tour when I trained her. No wonder I don't get Christmas cards from any of her former competitors today! Martina took the trophies, money, and the other players' places in history, by doing her homework and being open to change.

Unlike basketball players and coaches who traditionally have scouted each player's and team's tendencies by watching film, in preparation for upcoming games, tennis players during the 1980s just went out and played. I decided to take what I had learned from basketball about preparation and started going to Martina's opponents' matches. I would chart each stroke and note which shot each player would use on the court for every point. Did she like to go down the line, the high side of the net when hitting inside the court? Or if the ball was hit cross-court to her and she was behind on the baseline, did she like to respond by hitting cross-court back? How did she choose to play a certain point? What was her strength, the forehand or the backhand? All vital information when you are studying your opponent and figuring out a game plan to be successful.

Then Martina and I would look at previous matches and how her opponents had played against her. We had a book on many of the top players, just like baseball pitchers do against the hitters they face.

I remember being in Stuttgart, Germany, when Martina played Tracy Austin in the Porsche Tennis Grand Prix Tournament, in 1982. I had done the scouting, and when Martina played Tracy in the finals, she beat her 6–3, 6–3 in about 40 minutes. At the press conference after the match, Tracy was asked how she had gotten beat so easily. She answered incredulously, "It was like she knew where my shots were going before I even hit them." Our preparation paid off. Martina won a beautiful custom Porsche convertible, and I looked good driving it around Dallas for many years after—although it was a killer on gas!

Whether your opponent is the manager in the next office or the smaller, nimbler company that's coming out with a product similar to yours, you have to stay one step ahead and continually be ready to adjust your game to win over theirs. My motto has always been that even on my worst day I should *still* be better than my opponent on his or her best day! You have to set a standard for yourself in regard to preparation. This play focuses on how to do just that: by gathering useful information about your opponents and, quite frankly, about yourself, as well. I have always been upfront with my team and/or colleagues: I need to know how they play/work under pressure.

In addition to knowing your opponent, you also need to know your environment. Days after announcing that he was coming back to golf after a personal scandal that rocked the sports world, Tiger Woods was seen practicing. He played a round of golf at Augusta

National Golf Club in preparation for the prestigious event. Would Tiger just show up and take his chances on the day the tournament started, and play the course for the first time in a year? Of course not. Instead, he turned up a few weeks early for several practice rounds, to identify the trouble spots and the lay of the putting greens, and to strategize how he planned to avoid the water or the sand trap on each hole. You need to do the same thing when you start a new job, transfer to a new office, call on a new client, or simply take on a new responsibility. What is the lay of the land on *your* course? Where are the trouble spots? The tough holes? The sand traps? To thrive, not just survive, in the corporate environment, you have to prepare. By running your own scouting report, you can use what you've learned to strengthen your own performance and that of your company.

Homework comes in so many different forms these days—about your industry, your competitors, or trends in the market. If you have a feeling that a certain strategy might work, research it. In my opinion, homework also requires that you make phone calls and ask people who've walked a similar road what *they've* done in similar situations. When I prepare to broadcast games for ESPN or Fox Sports, I don't hesitate to call the coach of the team I am about to be covering, the team's last opponent's head coach, assistant coaches, and players I know on the team. All of these people are willing to share information and game plans—really. A tip: Call the person who put the scouting report or the presentation together. He or she has already done the research and will have the most information to share with you.

I'm a visual person, so my preparation and homework usually come together in a visual presentation. We have a saying in the world of sports: *Film never lies.* I've found that when I attempt to teach players by showing them film, they tend not to become very involved in what they're being shown if they're not in it. They're tying their shoes, scratching their heads, adjusting their shorts—anything but watching the screen. But the minute I show a clip that features them, they are locked in and paying attention—*because it's about them.* It's an interesting, and very human, character trait. Individuals don't see the crowd or the coach, the ball or opponent; instead, they lock in on what *they're* doing. Narcissism, when it takes this form, isn't all bad; occasionally, it can even be a great teaching tool.

Keep this in mind when you're presenting your homework to your team: You have to involve every team member in the presentation to really get buy-in. That's not to say you can't present a broad picture; just be sure to also include something for each team member. When I was coaching in Detroit, we would present a two-minute video specifically for each player before each game. It would include maybe 45 seconds on the opponent she would be guarding, and the rest of the time would be dedicated to the player herself, with highlights to build her up. We wanted to show the players the challenge—the opponents—while providing key points to remember, and then show them what they had done well in the past that would work in the situation. This technique helps people to clearly visualize success.

Likewise, seeing *yourself* succeed is an important part of doing your homework. You can apply this same technique to your team when you are going to make any presentation. Video is a valuable tool. Watching and listening to yourself—acknowledging your strong points and recognizing your weak points—is one of the best ways to edit, find room for improvements, and then make them.

Homework really hasn't changed from the time you were a kid in school. You just need to apply this habit to an adult situation. The process is the same: You learn something in school and you go home with assignments about the lesson. Your teacher expects you to put time, energy, and concentration into the subject. You solve problems, which you might have to do as they're unfolding in front of you, by simultaneously thinking on your feet and organizing your thoughts. Finally, you come back the next day and present what you've learned in a coherent form.

Homework can come in a variety of formats. Seek new opportunities when you can, and go outside if you can't get what you need internally. As a parent, like many of you, I try to be all things to all people, so I understand about feeling overwhelmed. Don't be afraid to outsource what you can. Thanks to today's technologies, we can get a lot of things done in a lot of places using the smart phones in our hands. If my assistant, Theresa, doesn't come in the office one day, or leaves early, she can still answer e-mail on her PDA. It's important to be flexible when you're trying to get all of your homework done! Let someone on your staff take his or her work home with when that person's kid has a game. Trust that he or she will get it done without you standing over his or her shoulder. Remember, it's not the quantity of the hours, but the quality. If you're fast and good and finish your work, it's okay to leave. You don't have to sit there until the 5:30 horn goes off. This isn't Bedrock, and we're not Barney and Fred waiting for the whistle. Now, if we're working on a project that's on a tight deadline, I'll expect you to stay late! The point is, it's a huge mistake to sit idle.

I remember having a conversation with an athlete friend of mine and several corporate representatives regarding the creation of a partnership with a multilevel marketing company. The athlete and his business partner were used to dealing with traditional corporate America, as opposed to multilevel marketing, and were not familiar with the latter concept. The reality, however, is that there's a lot of money to be made using both models. The tendency for many of us is to get stuck with what we know; in this case, my buddy was unable to see the benefits of this new kind of partnership. He knew and was comfortable with one business model, and therefore couldn't see the other ways to do business. That attitude could have jeopardized a potentially profitable, seven-figure deal, so what I said to him after hearing both sides was, *do your homework*. Research multilevel marketing, and find out what it's all about. Sometimes you can't see the big picture because you are clouded by what you already know. You need new information, a new perspective, to open your mind to newer and bigger possibilities. If you think you know everything about someone or some situation, I'll bet you don't! Test yourself. Look for a different interpretation, a new fact or figure. Trust me—it's out there!

Business is a matrix environment. Think of interlocking your fingers to make a platform of strength. There is a wealth of talent around you, and you can achieve greatness together by constructing a matrix that uses all of your strengths. Be open-minded about differences between people, and to innovative ideas, *especially* in difficult economic times. Those differences and new ideas can put you in a position of strength and inspire creativity that will get you noticed.

A Little Test

Read this sentence out loud:

> FINISHED FILES ARE THE RESULT OF YEARS OF SCIENTIFIC STUDY COMBINED WITH THE EXPERIENCE OF MANY YEARS.

Now, count the F's in the sentence.

Are you sure? Read it again, and count one more time. Did you get a different number?

In most cases, the first time people read this sentence, they will count either three or four F's. Then, when they slow down, read it again, and study it, they will see the "hidden" F's in the three "OF's" in the sentence. There are actually six F's in that sentence. When you read it out loud, those F's sound like V's. It's a fun little brain-teaser.

My friend Wes Lockard gave me a card with that sentence on it in 1976, and I've carried it around in my wallet ever since to illustrate the following point: You can be so focused on what you *think* you know that you forget to study, to do your homework, and remain open to learning something new. Perception is not always reality. Put in a little effort to peel away the layers and get to the truth.

Google It!

As I said, you have to be open-minded, because there are so many ways to view pretty much *anything* that life presents to you. There's a saying: "How do you eat an elephant?" The answer, of course, is, "Piece by piece." Information is so easily accessible these days. Go online, type your topic into Google, and you'll find a tutorial, a video, an article—the results are astonishing. When I'm faced with a subject I know little or nothing about, I can Google it from my phone. Here's an example: I was at Muhammad Ali's Celebrity Fight Night in Phoenix, in 2010, and I heard people around me whispering, "There's Sam Moore!" Now, I could see Randy Jackson from *American Idol*; songwriter David Foster, the so-called hit man because he's written so many hit songs; Jerry Weintraub, producer of *Ocean's Eleven, Twelve*, and *Thirteen*; actress Bo Derek; country diva Reba McEntire; and comedian and actor Chris Tucker. Yet with all of these celebrities there, the only person everyone seemed to be talking about was this guy Sam Moore. Was I the only person who didn't know who he was? So I Googled him right then and there, and found this (and much more) about him:

> **Samuel David Moore was an American R&B singer, best known as the tenor vocalist for Sam & Dave, considered by some the most successful and critically acclaimed duo in soul music history. Nicknamed "Soul Man" for the Grammy Award-winning song of the same name, Moore was named to the Rock & Roll Hall of Fame, the Grammy Hall of Fame (for "Soul Man"), and the Vocal Group Hall of Fame. In 2008, Rolling Stone Magazine named Moore one of the 100 greatest singers of the rock era (1950s–2008).**

Okay, he's the "Soul Man" guy—as in "I'm a soul man . . . ," as in the Blues Brothers. I asked my mother who Sam Moore was, and she replied in two words: "Soul Man."

The Internet can connect you quickly and easily, from just about anywhere in the world today, to the information you need—or you can always ask your mother. Either way, there's no excuse for not having the information you need to do your homework. Find out what you need to know on the company, the people in it, the market, and the environment. Find out everything. Google the people; Google yourself! Learn about the environment and get the scouting report.

I can't emphasize enough the importance of familiarizing yourself with the environment. If you're going to Philly, find out about the cheese steak. Take a cue from rock stars and bands. Did you know that they spell out the name of the city they're performing in with tape in front of them on the stage? That way they don't say, "Thank you Detroit!" when they're in Topeka.

If you don't find out about your environment before you get there, you will no doubt learn about it the hard way—usually, by making some major faux pas. This is especially true when it comes to international business. Richard Gere once repeatedly kissed Indian actress Shilpa Shetty on the cheek at an AIDS awareness rally in New Delhi, India, a country where public displays of affection are a *big* no-no. Afterward, an Indian court issued a warrant for his arrest, and irate protestors burned effigies of him in the streets. Though the warrant was later suspended, I think you see the point: learn a little, or a lot, about the people you are going to be spending time with so that you will know what behavior is acceptable to them, what makes them comfortable, and what might motivate them to turn you into a voodoo doll and poke your image with pins.

Doing your homework can be as basic as remembering someone's name so that you can use it in conversation, especially when you see the person the next time. If your memory isn't great, write down what you need to remember. Make yourself flashcards. Write it on the palm of your hand, if that's what it takes. My "play" is to say people's names, look them in the eye, and try to associate them with where I met them. If I don't say their names out loud—as in, "Nice to meet you, Cheryl. Great to see you here at the Mavs game"—

chances are I won't have the recall later. I am fully aware of this weakness on my part, so I make sure to follow up after meeting someone and receiving his or her business card. As soon as I have a minute to myself, I write on the card where I met the person. I then usually send him or her a short "nice to meet you" e-mail.

When I coach, I keep all of the necessary information I might need—every possible situation, point, and counterpoint—on index cards, held together with a rubber band. As you can tell, it's a pretty sophisticated system. In the NFL, you'll see coaches carrying clipboards with laminated sheets. It's essentially the same thing, though—just a way to keep track of their research and have it close at hand. When the camera comes in their direction, however, they hide their boards, because they hold their cheat sheets, their strategies.

You can do a version of the same thing in meetings; you don't have to memorize everything. Put the main points of your agenda on a cheat sheet of your own devising—whatever works for you. At ESPN, we hold papers that we call "rundowns" or "shot sheets" in our hands or on the desk in front of us. They provide readily available information so that we can better communicate with the viewers. I recommend you design a cheat sheet for your next business meeting or presentation to help keep you on track; and remember to keep it simple—you're supposed to talk about A, B, and C. Though you might not end up needing this visual aid, it never hurts to have it on hand; just knowing it's there will give you confidence.

Scouting Report

Everything in sports can be reduced to numbers. You can re-create a whole game in your mind just by looking at the box scores. You can break down the weaknesses of your home team and the opponent. You can track a record or a streak and figure out who's your best bet. You can do this in business, too, using the annual report or the balance sheet. For example, Warren Buffett's company, Berkshire Hathaway, produces an annual report that tracks its performance against the S&P 500—not just for the year of the report, but for every year since 1965. Talk about expectations. People don't expect Warren Buffett to lose when they look at that track record. They expect him and his board to win.

Doing your homework is also about commitment. It's about putting in the time and not being lazy. You are paying a price for your success with your time, so calculate how successful you want to be. A half-hour's worth? That won't get you too far into retirement. Success is about preparation and training. If you train hard, you will improve in anything you do, from typing to running sprints to making sales. You might not end up being able to outrun Olympic champion and world's fastest man Usain Bolt, but you will be able to reach individual goals and achieve your personal best.

I get excited when I'm learning about other people and other companies. I read a lot of biographies, because I like to see how successful men and women started out and what their road to success looked like. I've found there's a common thread running through most of their stories: They practiced, trained, and did their homework. They didn't cut corners. They found good partners and they understood how surrounding themselves with the right people could make them better.

If you're not willing to put the time into research, you will be the weak link on your team. It's that simple. It's a basic component of being competitive: You have to be an asset, not the weight pulling everyone else down. If you're going to do something, do it to the best of your ability. You're in control of that—always.

See the Future

You have to create the future. What I mean by that is that doing your homework is not always about today or tomorrow, but farther into the future. Innovative and progressive people think ahead. Sam Wyly drove this point home in his book *$1,000 and an Idea: Entrepreneur to Billionaire* (Brilliance Audio, 2008). Sam founded a computer services company in 1963—when hardly anyone had computers. Called University Computing Company, the company served engineers, scientists, and researchers. By the time the word "Internet" appeared in the *Oxford English Dictionary*, in 1974, Sam's company was charting more than $125 million in annual sales. Sam Wyly was looking ahead. He was thinking ahead. He kept his eye on the prize, building his company right then and there while trying to figure out how he was going to create and be a part of change. That's an important part of preparation: seeing what you're going to need *tomorrow* to succeed.

Larry Fitzgerald Provides a Lesson on Observing

If there's one thing I know, it's that although I might not be the best women's basketball player in the world anymore, everyone I play against will agree that I still compete hard and have a love for the game.

Larry Fitzgerald will attest to this. Larry is an All-Pro wide receiver for the NFL's Arizona Cardinals. Here's a guy who was born a few years after I graduated from Old Dominion, in 1983. Do the math: I was a few years older than him. One day when I was in Phoenix, we played a little one-on-one at Lifetime Fitness. Beforehand, I watched him for a few minutes. Every time he was going to drive to shoot, he would dribble with his left hand to get a rhythm. *That's* doing research—on the spot. I figured out exactly when he was going to shoot. Just by watching him, I recognized a pattern. I used that information to try to take away his comfort dribble, going to his left. I attempted to force him to do something uncomfortable, by making him go to his right.

Later, he asked me how I knew to guard him that way, and I told him, "I watched you. When you shoot, you always put the ball in your left hand, so I tried to take away your strength and send you to a weakness."

Larry and I connected because he realized I was observing him as it was happening. Here we were, two different athletes, two different agendas, yet able to develop a mutual respect for another.

You can make that same kind of connection in *any* situation—business, personal, play. Break things down and look for an advantage. Figure out how, at 51, I was going to stop Larry, at 26, or at least compete with him. (After I finish writing this book, I'm going to check the birth certificates just to be sure.) Never forget, there's always someone behind you or in front of you who is faster or stronger, or who has more business experience or product know-how. But if you're willing to make the effort and do the grunt work, it will pay off.

Larry, by the way, paid me an amazing compliment after that pickup game. He went on Twitter, where he tweeted: "I played with Nancy Lieberman, the best women's basketball player ever. She can ball." That tweet went all over the world, and it really made me feel good that he respected and admired me. Larry is the best receiver in the NFL, with the best hands. But I admire him just as much for his work ethic and the way he continues to prepare for success, when he is already near the top of his game.

We can all experience that feeling of triumph by preparing ourselves and being observant—by doing our homework. That was a "wow" moment for me. I affected Larry's life, and made an impression. That's what hard work does for us. It holds us—and others—to higher standards.

Plays to Remember

- *Do your homework!* Your preparation will enable you to outperform the competition.

- *Be open-minded.* There are many roads to success.

- *Ask questions.* The only "bad" question is the one you don't ask.

8

Stay in Shape

If you don't have time to do it right, when will you have time to do it over?

—JOHN WOODEN, HALL OF FAME BASKETBALL COACH

Why was I able to play for nine minutes in a WNBA pro basketball game at age 50 and not make a fool of myself? Because I've kept myself in shape.

Even after I retired from basketball, I worked out on a regular basis because I like to feel good about myself. I was taught early on in life that my body was my temple, and I always took that seriously. I've made sure, to the best of my ability, that I don't abuse my body. I respect it and do everything possible to defy time and gravity (which, sadly, is ultimately a losing battle!).

There are so many things that we can't control when it comes to our health. However, we do each have the ability to do something positive for ourselves by eating right and staying in shape. When you feel good about yourself physically—if you're healthy and not dragging or tired—you feel like you can take on the world. That's why the health and beauty business is a multibillion-dollar—and growing—segment of the market—few among us are not trying to look and feel better. Why? Because when we look better, we feel better. Perception *does* become reality, in most cases. Think about it this way: If you're willing to put in the hours at the office to achieve success, you need to do the same with your health and appearance.

I make it a point to do something athletic every day, whether it's walking outside, getting on the treadmill or exercise bike, or playing basketball, golf, or tennis—anything that will burn some calories. We're talking simple math here: If you take in more calories than you expend, you will have a more difficult time staying in shape. A 2010 study published in the *Journal of the American Medical*

Association found that women who consume a *normal* diet need 60 minutes of moderate exercise *every day* to prevent weight gain as they age. These recommendations were more than double the guidelines of the federal government at that time, which had suggested 30 minutes of moderate exercise five days a week. Honestly, I wasn't surprised by the new findings, not when I think of the women I know and how hard it is for them to maintain their weight through middle age and menopause.

Doing something active every day doesn't mean you have to work out like a world-class athlete. It just means choosing a healthy lifestyle. Do it for *you*. I know so many women—chances are, you're one of them—who spend all of their energy doing things for others. They spread themselves so thin between the demands of work, home, and family that they neglect themselves. Bring the focus back to *you*. Make it a priority to take time for yourself; schedule it into your day, every day. I'm a pretty busy gal myself, between taking care of my son and work. I also travel about 100,000 miles a year. So, to allot time for myself, I try to get up in the morning about a half hour before my son does. I make breakfast, spend time with him, watch some television, and we talk about what's happening that day for each of us. When he goes out the front door to catch the school bus, I head to the health club. Some days I work out on my own; other days, I rely on my personal trainer, Brian Darden, to be my accountability partner. Just like you, I need to be pushed on days that I'm just not feeling up to it. It's a good idea to have somebody on your health "team," whether it's a trainer or a friend, to keep you going when all you want to do is make excuses. I know I have to show up when I have scheduled Brian to be at the club to work out with me.

You will not be gung-ho every day, but every day *is* another chance to strengthen your body. There are mornings when I'm sore and my knees hurt, so I don't run, but ride a bike instead. On the days that I do feel good, I work harder, run faster, and throw in more cardio. There are *countless* ways to get in shape. Some people prefer taking classes, in yoga, body-sculpting, hip-hop dancing, or so-called boot camps. Work out with a partner—business or personal. Trust me, there's some form of exercise out there for you—so get out there and exercise your right to be healthy.

Make a Commitment and Get Started

Start by making a commitment to work out for the next 120 days. Here are some tips for those first months:

- If you want to build your endurance, add cardio.
- If you're interested in shaping your body, add weights.
- Give up sweets, or chips, or alcohol for this period of time.
- Concentrate on making one change on the "calories in" side and one on the "calories out" side.

I promise you, you won't believe what you will look like by investing 120 days, just by carving out an hour even three or four days a week. I guarantee that after these four months, you will be more confident and have a more positive outlook. Your mind-set is going to be different, too. You will begin to exude an aura of positive self-esteem, which everyone around you is going to notice. And it's going to be *real*, because you have made the commitment and invested the time. You'll be amazed at the number of people who will look at you in admiration and wonder what you've been doing. If they're smart, they'll ask, so that they can start doing the same thing themselves!

I've been a spokesperson for a nutritional company called Mannatech for many years; both my son and I use its products. One year, I was scheduled to speak at the company's national convention, and when I saw CEO Sam Caster come in, I couldn't believe how great he looked. He had lost weight, was wearing flattering clothes, and had a real swagger in his walk. He knew he looked good; it was as if he had an aura surrounding him. It struck me that it was because he'd been taking care of himself.

It's hard, if not impossible, to successfully lead a company or a family if you're tired, cranky, and out of shape. Think of it this way: Taking care of yourself is just another way that you can be a role model. You can increase your company's overall health by setting your own personal standard, by showing your team that exercising and eating right should play a defining role in *their* everyday lives, as well. Simply put, if you don't take care of your body, over time you will become increasingly tired, both emotionally and physically, and that will have a negative impact on your effectiveness with your team.

Now I'm not going to pitch a diet here; there are quantities of information already out there on that topic. But I will tell you what *I* do. If I know on a particular day that I'm not going to be able to work out, I simply don't eat as much. And I eat more protein and fewer carbohydrates on those low-activity days, because I don't want my body to get confused and store the fat. I pay attention to foods that most of us tend to forget are really high in calories, like fruit juice. I like juices, but since I try to limit my liquid calories, I dilute them with water. You can't ever go wrong with water; in fact, I drink it as if I were a camel.

It's all about having some discipline. For example, I was born eating licorice. I love it, and I will never give it up. But because I don't eat 10 rolls coated with butter at every meal, and I don't put globs of dressing on my salads, I can have my licorice. An important rule is always to practice moderation; then when you go down a dress size or a waist size and find an outfit that looks really good on you, use that as incentive to keep taking those steps.

By all means, don't starve yourself—*please*. It will confuse your body. Even if you're taking baby steps in cutting back on certain foods, don't go to extremes. Simply dedicate yourself to eating right on more days than you splurge.

Even though I'm a professional athlete, and training is a big part of who I am and what I do, I'm also an overworked mom who has to prioritize to find time to remain fit. I do it, however, not only because I want to look good and be physically healthy, but also because my workouts are vital to my *mental health*. They are something I do for *me*, a time that is mine alone, when I can disconnect from the demands and stresses that are a part of my daily life (and that I'm sure are part of yours, as well). Which brings me to my next point . . .

Minimize Stress

Managing stress is an inherent characteristic of the business world. Here's a tip for relieving stress: Focus on taking care of yourself, for this will translate into improved performance in the boardroom, no matter what you do for a living.

It's not always easy to motivate yourself to hit the gym, particularly when you're on the road and just want to veg in your hotel room, sleep in an extra hour, or when you're so swamped with work that you absolutely *need* to spend that extra hour in the office to catch up. Keep in mind, however, those are the times when it's most important to push yourself to take care of yourself. Encouraging yourself to do something difficult—work out, solve a conflict, or confront a challenge—defines who you are and what you will be. This is so important for women today!

This may well be the reason that studies frequently find that two-thirds of female business executives and 75 percent of *all* chief executives exercise regularly. Remember that Oppenheimer Funds survey I told you about in the first chapter? Eighty-one percent of the senior female executives surveyed said they participated in some sort of physical activity, sport, or exercise, most of them at least three times a week. These executives also said that they thought women who participated in sports made more productive employees, and were more highly respected by their fellow employees.

Regular exercise pays off in more ways than maintaining your health and stamina: It helps keep you focused and disciplined, and strengthens your self-confidence. Research also shows that the quality of work, mental performance, and time management improves

65 percent or more on the days people exercise, compared with the days they don't.

It's certainly no secret that people who are attractive and maintain a healthy weight are more likely to be successful in the workplace. A report from the Federal Reserve Bank of St. Louis found that women who had what the report defined as "below-average looks" tended to earn an average of 8 percent less per hour than "above-average-looking" employees, while those with "above-average looks" tended to earn 4 percent more an hour more than those with "average looks." Another study, this one sponsored by the National Bureau of Economic Research, found that every 1 percent increase in body mass in women resulted in a 0.6 percent drop in family income.

Still, everyone needs a "treat" once in awhile, right? In my case, I try to reward myself with health-related activities, such as going for a facial, manicure, pedicure, or massage. During this downtime, I can totally relax, turn off my phone, and use the time to restore my energy and focus. It's absolutely essential to create some personal space just for you. At first, you might feel guilty doing this, but *do it anyway*.

Speaking of phones, we're all *far* too attached to our iPhones and BlackBerrys. How many times have you been engaged in a conversation and you hear your phone and immediately become distracted from what you were talking about? It's a common reaction. Way too many of us have become addicted to the contraptions that are supposed to keep us connected and on top of things, and we forget to *connect to ourselves* every once in awhile. So turn it off! Give it— and your mind—a rest.

A Few Words for Women Only

There are some basic differences between men and women when it comes to health and performance. As many women have come to notice, when they work or live together in close proximity— in offices, on sports teams, in college dorms, or even with close friends—their menstrual cycles tend to sync up. Why? The simple answer is hormones and the human instinct to reproduce. The hormones of those around you affect your own hormone production. Biologically, the way to ensure maximum reproduction in a herd is to create the maximum number of opportunities for reproduction—that is, to have the entire group of females fertile at the same time. Thus, a woman producing hormones during her fertile period will jump-start other women's bodies into becoming fertile. This doesn't happen immediately; it may take a few months of working or living together.

With this in mind, just imagine a roomful of angry premenstrual women together trying to get something done—whether it's winning a basketball game or hitting a sales target. It complicates matters. But it's a reality, and it's one that men don't have to deal with.

I remember when one of my best players in Detroit totally broke down after we had lost in overtime to the world-champion Houston Comets, in front of 14,000 people. I was *so* proud of my players, an expansion team that hadn't been expected to get that far. I'm thinking, "Wow, she's really taking this loss hard." All of a sudden, she started crying, and said, "I miss my fiancé." "What?!," I asked. "I miss him *so* badly," she repeated. I had prepared a powerful postgame speech and had already launched into it, but in this moment of heightened estrogen I had to stop my speech to go over and hug this player. I'm making light of the moment, but it was very real. There's nothing in the procedure manual that would have prepared me for it, either.

How do we deal with this very real part of being women? We have to recognize what's going on. If you or a teammate or coworker is agitated or seems overly emotional or irrational, stop for a minute and consider what might be going on. Be understanding and try to find a solution. The solution might well be to find some Motrin, give some to your coworker, and say, "Let's get on with our job."

Menopause is a whole other issue, especially for women in leadership positions. Women going through menopause or perimenopause (the years prior to menopause) often report experiencing a variety of cognitive issues, including fatigue, memory problems, irritability, and rapid mood swings. Here, again, the causes are hormone-related, which can then cause real-life problems for women. Consider a top-level female executive in a decision-making position who has suddenly begun to have trouble remembering things—a woman formerly known for being quick and decisive, or the company's memory bank.

I have many friends who are now dealing with this, and I try to help them through it with humor. One friend in particular was experiencing nonstop hot flashes. It seemed like every time we were in a meeting, she'd take a piece of paper and start fanning herself. I joked that it was as if she was having her own personal summers. It was my way of making light of it, while indicating I understood what she was going through. I'd say, for example, "Hey, Cindy, where did you go just then? The Bahamas? Turks and Caicos?" She even began to have fun with it. She started referring to her hot flashes as "taking a vacation." Every time she got a hot flash, she'd name it after a place she had gone to or wanted to visit. She developed quite an array of locales—everywhere from Chile to Africa and many in between. She'd call me up and say, "Hey Nancy, I'm adding to my travel list: Borneo—it's the third largest island in the world."

Believe it or not, menopause is a major workplace issue these days, and it's not going away anytime soon. As baby boomers continue to age it is going to become virtually pervasive through at least 2020. Better, then, when it happens to you, to think of it as a voyage, and figure out what you can and can't change when it comes to "the Change." Of course, there are medical remedies, and you can talk to your doctor about those. But what about just layering your clothing? Or bring an electric fan to work? The one thing you cannot do is allow menopause to control your life. Confront it, get informed, and attack it.

Another problem that seems almost inevitable with menopause is that women will begin to gain weight. Forewarned is forearmed: Deal with it early. It will be much easier to face that weight gain if you start from a place of strength. Get lean and mean *before* you hit the menopause years. Don't live in the past, trying to get into some size-two dress; prepare for the future instead. For example, I used to be really fast on my feet. I'm not as quick now. I have to deal with that by working on the skills I *can* hold onto—my shot, my agility, and my ability to prepare for my opponents. Getting a handle on both menopause and your menstrual cycle will help you gain a sense of balance and normalcy—instead of malice for everybody in your way. Don't let either of these hormonal realities—or any change that life throws at you, for that matter—hinder your performance or how you're perceived. Instead, prepare, gather knowledge, and understand your situation, so that you can cope with it constructively.

Plays to Remember

- *Make you a priority.* A healthy you is a successful you.

- *Do the math.* Calories in, calories out. When it comes to diet and exercise, be consistent with eating and exercise. I'm never on a diet; the way I eat is a way of life. If I want to lose some weight, I burn more calories.

- *Change will happen.* Be prepared for it.

9

Sports Talk

Make sports a part of your business conversations and then marvel that something so simple can infiltrate the hearts of the toughest men in the world and create an instantaneous relationship.

—NANCY LIEBERMAN

I've emphasized repeatedly throughout this book that you don't have to have been an athlete to benefit in the workplace from the lessons sports can teach. In this chapter, this play, we'll take that concept one step further. It's time to become more involved with sports overall—whether as a spectator or a player—so that you can participate more fully in your office "sports talk."

You don't have to be a star athlete to play golf or tennis recreationally, or even to work out at a gym. Participating in these activities at any level will give you your own personal sports vocabulary, as well as a level of knowledge that will help you find common ground among business contacts and colleagues. What's more, you'll enjoy how you look and feel as a result of your hard work and commitment. And as an interested spectator, you'll find yourself more accepted as part of the team when office talk turns to the playoff games.

For starters, get involved when the March Madness pool e-mail goes out. Go online and buy some tickets to sporting events, then use them as an opportunity to spend some quality time with your boss and other decision makers. By now, you no doubt are aware that sports often are a key component of workplace camaraderie. It's time to use it to *your* advantage.

Use the Morning Headlines

Approach the morning sports headlines as a research project. Pull out the sports section of *USA Today* or your local paper, and read some of the articles in it. At the very least, be aware which sports are in season and when things in each particular sport are heating up—in particular, when it's time for the playoffs. Hey, you never know, you might even develop an interest in it.

A really good way to get involved is to choose a favorite player in each sport or team, follow him or her, and dig a little deeper. Where did he or she go to college? Did he or she participate in the Olympics? A little trivia dropped conveniently into workplace conversations can go a long way.

Another tip: Sports is all about the numbers—records, streaks, wins/losses—and sports fans freakishly remember a lot of these, including, I'm sure, many of the men you work with. Make the "stats" fun; see if you can stump your coworkers, especially the diehard fans.

Use Tickets as a Tool

Tickets can be a great equalizer in the business world. I knew a councilwoman in Ames, Iowa, who felt like she was on her own private island because she was never included in casual conversations at work. She started to realize that the guys around her were all talking about sports and she wanted to find a way to become part of their group. Here's how she "played" it: She came into the office one day and made it known that she had season tickets for the Iowa State Cyclones football team and the local AA baseball team. Then she casually offered them to a couple of the guys: "Bill, I can't go to the game on Friday; do you want my tickets?"

It was remarkable how soon she became part of the loop. The same guys who never seemed interested in spending time or sharing information with this woman were now acting like her buddies, all because she had used her sports tickets as a tool to become part of their group. Soon they were asking her if she wanted to go join them to catch a game on television or have a beer. Simply by purchasing two sets of season tickets, she was made part of the pack.

Tickets to various sporting events also can give you an edge over others by serving as a unique calling card. Let's say, for example, you go into a business meeting and aren't sure what to leave behind—a brochure, a business card, a DVD—why not leave tickets to a game? You better believe you'll be remembered, for a variety of reasons. First, it will keep the conversation going, because the people who receive and use your tickets will want to thank you. Second, you'll be in the position of giver rather than taker—always the stronger position. Finally, in many cases, you will be the recipient of some kind of return-the-favor gesture. But even if you aren't, on the simplest level, your gift will certainly differentiate you from other business associates and help potential clients remember who you are.

An even better idea is to ask someone to join you and your friends at a game. Sitting through a sporting event, and sharing a drink or a bite to eat before or after, can have a memorable effect on someone you're looking to impress. You'll be pleasantly surprised how well a client or colleague will remember you the next time you call.

In sum, you can use the sports connection to cut through all the defined lines of hierarchy—there is, after all, no organizational chart at basketball, football, or baseball games. There, everyone, regardless of rank or income, is a fan, making it easier to forge stronger friendships later in the workplace.

Strike Up the Conversation

When I say that it's time to "talk sports," I'm really just trying to encourage you to step out of the comfort zone in which many women have lived for many years in regard to how they've done business. It's for a very good reason that every chapter of this book is full of sports analogies. I've also included a glossary at the back that defines various sports terms within the context of a business. Refer to it to help you better communicate, motivate, and lead the people who work with you and/or for you. Using these terms, as I've mentioned earlier, can be great icebreakers with people you don't know.

A few years ago, my best friend, Wes, told me that a dear friend of his, named Mike, was dying of cancer. I wanted to do something for Mike, and I knew he was a huge Pittsburgh Steelers fan. Wes told me that giving Mike something from his favorite team would make him smile. So I cold-called Dave Lockett, the communications coordinator for the Pittsburgh Steelers, introduced myself (I didn't know if he knew who I was), and explained why I was calling. We immediately bonded while talking about Mike's condition and the fact that he loved the Steelers. I asked Dave if he would be kind enough to ask Steelers quarterback Ben Roethlisberger to autograph a picture and send it to Mike.

Dave and I must have stayed on the phone for 40 minutes reminiscing about sports. In no time I felt like I had known him my whole life. Later, not only did he send an autographed picture of Ben Roethlisberger to Mike at his home, but he added an autographed football and some other Steelers memorabilia. When Mike's wife brought the Steelers "goody basket" to him at the hospital, she said she hadn't seen her husband smile like that in months. Later, when Mike died, he was buried with all of the memorabilia.

I can say without any hesitation that was the best cold call I ever made. To this day, though Dave Lockett and I still have never met in person, we talk every five or six months. Our bond is as strong as if we had been friends living close to each other in the same city for 20 years.

Stories such as these are interesting, even heartwarming, but they aren't the most important point I'm trying to make here. What's essential is the message they highlight—that is, how incredibly vital the world of sports can be to your success, if you learn how to use them. Sports are humanizing. They make people forget—even for just a minute—how brilliant you might be, how many awards you might have won, and how much money you make. By including sports as part your business conversations, I am convinced you'll soon discover how something so simple can infiltrate the hearts of the toughest businessmen in the world—and forge relationships, instantaneously. I know; I have lived this.

Because I can banter back and forth about sports with the guys, I have formed friendships with some pretty unlikely candidates. Take my friend Arizona Cardinals All-Pro wide receiver Larry Fitzgerald. After knowing him all of two days, we soon were chattering like old pals, via text message, using sports to connect. When I told Larry that I planned to use him as an example of excellence in my book, he shot back that he would pick up a copy to show support. Then he reminded me that his confidence had been at an all-time high since beating me in a three-point shooting contest. To which I told him that he was "done" the next time I got him on the court, and that I had just been nice to him the last time, that I had let him beat me. I also offered to send him the basketball instructional book I had written years ago to help him work on his game. I closed by asking: "By the way, didn't I beat you at horse?" He fired back, "Put your money where your mouth is, Nancy. You don't have what it takes. You're a coach now."

My feelings weren't hurt, of course, because I could tell, even via texting, that what he was really saying was, "I like you. You're fun. You're one of us." I can take it and I can dish it out, and our friendship will grow because of it.

As I've said before, you don't necessarily have to *play* sports with someone in your office to develop this kind of friendly back-and-forth exchange. It can be a fan rivalry: Maybe you like the Red Sox and he backs the Yankees; or perhaps your two favorite college teams (or alma maters) are facing off against one another in a big game. It might even be based on a Final Four or Super Bowl bet. The bottom line is that it's about communicating on another level, one that's fun. Lighten it up; use a little humor and friendly sarcasm. Trust me, it's endearing—especially when you do it to them before they do it to you!

I know that a lot of you are working hard to get ahead, but you don't have to be so tightly wound to move forward. You don't have to be perfect, either; you just want people to truly like and respect you. Wouldn't you rather do business with someone who likes to have fun than someone who is always deadly serious? Remember the movie *Miss Congeniality*, with Sandra Bullock? Why did people like her? Because she was fun, and she knew how to joke around.

Stop taking yourself so seriously. Talking sports will help you "be real," at the same time you're sharing an opinion. It teaches you how to disagree amicably then get over the disagreement while maintaining respect for the other person. In fact, sports talk is great practice for those tough conversations you will have to have one day, about your raise, promotion, or time off. It also teaches you how to go to the wall for your teammates, and not leave them out there or throw them under the bus. If you demonstrate that kind of loyalty in a conversation about baseball, you can bet it will strengthen the relationship when it comes to real work situations, too.

Ultimately, you want to give people a reason to want to be around you, to respect you and like you. I have had so many men and women tell me—albeit, begrudgingly—that they admire me for my passion for the New York Yankees. Do I take a lot of heat about the Bronx Bombers? Yes, of course I do! No matter. I just fire back about the team's rich history of winning the World Series—27 times and counting. And, yes, I smile when I say that.

Learn to Tell a Story

There are businesspeople who are natural storytellers. They are comfortable telling stories about growing up or raising their kids in such a way to make you laugh or cry or make their point incredibly well. Other professionals may not be so willing to reveal personal details in a business setting. That's another reason why sports are so great to use for teaching analogies. I meet new people every day, and every day, just talking about sports immediately puts me on their level and gives me a way to relate to them. That's because every single day, another athletic event takes place somewhere—whether it's high school, college, or professional—providing us all with potential topics of conversation.

A female executive friend of mine named Sarah asked me one day, "Why do you always use these sports analogies? Why does it always have to be about sports? Not everyone cares about sports. Some people care about art or music." I explained to her that sports had taught me—and could teach her, as well—how to prepare for high-intensity situations in business. Sports are all about executing in the clutch, unlike any other activity (except maybe war, and war talk is not, in my opinion, a good motivator). Sports relay so many positive messages about performing under pressure, to both individuals and team members collectively. You win because you have prepared and practiced a skill over and over again. Participating in sports also teaches you how to visualize success, how to get there—all good lessons for business.

"Give me an example," Sarah demanded.

"Hitting the shot at the buzzer when I was a kid. Do you know how many times when I was playing in the schoolyard and, while dribbling, I'd talk to myself? 'Ten, nine—Lieberman goes left—eight, seven—she pulls right—six, five, four, three, two, one—the ball leaves her hand just before the buzzer—and it's good!' I had practiced that a thousand times before I experienced it in an actual game setting. I visualized myself doing that while I was lying in bed at night, daydreaming in school, and practicing in the park. 'Three, two, one—Lieberman with the shot! Yes, Nancy Lieberman hits the shot at the buzzer, and the Knicks win.' It was familiar."

I went on to explain to Sarah that sports can teach you how to prepare for every situation, and I've applied that to business. What do we do in practice? What's our contingency plan? These are two of the most important questions to ask, both on the court or field and in the office. You *have* to consider these scenarios, and practice for their eventual outcome. Every move should have a countermove and a change in strategy, enabling you to react while it's happening in real time. Sports are *always* relevant.

It's no surprise to me that both Warren Buffett and Bill Gates are fanatical bridge players. People around the world play bridge online against Warren, people who don't even know they're playing against Warren Buffett. It also doesn't surprise me that he considers sports an important part of his successful business strategy. He played high school basketball for a great coach, named Bob Dwyer, who later guided the boys' basketball team at Carroll High School in Washington, DC, to a legendary 55-game winning streak, from 1958 to 1960. Coach Dwyer told a young Warren Buffett not to take a shot unless he knew he was going to make it—a strategy that Warren declares he has always applied to his business principles.

The cross-reference of sports analogies to those of business is undeniable. Your quarterback is your "fearless leader"; your company is getting ready to make a big acquisition, and it's a "grand slam!"; your team leaders have put together a new portfolio for you to sell, and now "the ball's in your court," you're in control of your own destiny.

I have a mental library of great sports stories that I can use on different occasions. You can, too, even if it's just an anecdote about your son or daughter on the school court or field or the neighborhood pool. The objective is to come up with scenarios that everyone can identify with, so that you can find common ground upon which to stand and conduct business. By having these kinds of anecdotes ready, you will be well armed with icebreakers to share in real-life business settings. And remember, they don't have to be things you've experienced personally. I recall as a child reading about Lou Gehrig and Muhammad Ali, and applying lessons from their lives to my own. Use sports experiences for your gain, and to connect with people, even those you never imagined you could bond with.

Every day, you have an opportunity to find a story to add to your own mental library. They're in the sports section; they're called headlines. They will provide you with all the material you need to improve your communication skills. Instead of saying to yourself, "I have no idea what they're talking about, and I don't care," pick up the paper, listen to ESPN or the sports report on the nightly news. It takes only a small investment of your time, one that I know will pay off, big time.

Plays to Remember

- *Use tickets to sporting events as a tool for connecting and rewarding.* They will be a key reminder that you were there.

- *Tell a story.* You've lived, so you have stories to tell. Sports just make it more interesting for the listener.

- *Pay attention to headlines.* Read the local sports section or listen to the sports news once a day. Believe me, it's well worth your time.

10

Game Time!

If it doesn't matter who wins or loses, then why do they keep score?
—VINCE LOMBARDI, LEGENDARY FOOTBALL COACH

It was 1979 and I was in the locker room in Greensboro, North Carolina, putting on my Old Dominion uniform to play in the national championship game against Louisiana Tech. We had lost only one game that season up until that point, making us number one in the nation. I was the team leader, the one everybody looked to for calm and confidence, and the look in my eye said we were ready to play. But sitting there in the locker room, I had to admit to myself that I was nervous—*very* nervous. In fact, I was hyperventilating. My fingernails had turned blue, indicating I wasn't getting enough oxygen throughout my body. I was thinking, "This is *crazy*! This is where I've always wanted to be!" My team and I had worked so hard to get here, yet I had gotten so caught up in the hype of the championship game and all of the inherent pressure that surrounds it that it had become a huge problem. And at that moment I didn't know how to overcome it.

As we ran out on the court, I sensed that my teammates were noticing a difference in me. To tell the truth, I couldn't get my second wind. In contrast, Louisiana Tech came out with intensity and confidence and jumped all over us from the beginning. They took the lead and the momentum. By halftime, we were down by 12 points, and very much in jeopardy of getting blown out.

As I walked off the court and into the locker room for the half, I remember saying one of my favorite words—"really"—to myself: "Really, Nancy, are you *scared*? Are you scared of the moment? Everyone is depending on you, and you're letting them down."

The game was being broadcast on NBC, the first time a women's national championship game was shown live on national television. All I could think was that I was blowing it, big time. I was engaged in a mental battle with myself. I can remember standing in front of the mirror in the locker room, looking at myself, and reminding myself: "You've done this before. You've played in big games. You've played for championships. You've played for gold medals. You've played in the *Olympics.* And now you're screwing up because you're nervous?"

I then took a breath, to calm myself down. I was looking within myself for the deep confidence I had always displayed in such situations, not the false hope I was depending on at that time. When I went back on the floor for the second half, I was the old me, the me I knew—the calm, confident, ready-for-the-moment me.

In the huddle, before we went back out onto the court, I announced to my teammates that we were not leaving the floor without the championship trophy. "We *will* win," I said. "We are the better team, and we have worked for this moment." Different attitude, different leadership, different results. The second half brought a 22-point swing. We overcame the 12-point deficit, to win by 10 points, 75–65, and claim the first of two consecutive national championships.

It was game time, time to deliver the goods, and we did. Game time is your time to shine, to show people exactly what you can do. All the planning, meetings, hours of practice, and research that you've done in the preceding days, weeks, months, and sometimes even years, finally come to fruition. It's time to prove who you really are and how good you can be.

To shine, you have to execute with true leadership. There are countless qualities necessary to be a great leader, but I believe the most important requirement—in business or in sports—is integrity. Integrity is about being honest, consistent, fair, and just. It's about having people trust in your words and your deeds. To me, integrity also means having the determination, the staying power, to silence the critics.

To be a great leader, on game day and every day, you have to have integrity, take responsibility, and fight for unity among your team members. Leadership also is about taking ownership, and getting others to do the same. I'm big on team chemistry, so I always try to minimize roadblocks, disagreements, and dissention. Successful leaders sit back and observe; when there's a problem, they ponder before they speak. They might get angry, but they reflect and evaluate possible scenarios and solutions before deciding on the best approach to take.

A lot of women (men, too) resist confrontation. They'll do almost anything to avoid sitting down with someone face-to-face to make a bad situation right. In such circumstances, resist the temptation to react in a knee-jerk, overly emotional way, especially if you are mad; instead, take time to contemplate, to cool down. Confrontation does not always have to be a negative experience; it can simply take the form of a serious, heartfelt discussion with someone with whom you're having a problem. Remember, if a hammer is the only tool in your toolbox, you're in trouble.

You can't force someone to be responsible if he or she chooses to be unprepared and dodge his or her duties. You can, however, be prepared to manage the morale and the complications that are certain to arise *because* of that one person's lack of integrity. Business is always going to be contentious, because you're dealing with people, and people are complicated. I'm not a fan of managing by using fear tactics. I prefer to lead by example, by being fair but firm. If we're on the same team, I have an expectation of you; if you fail to meet that expectation, then we have a conflict. To resolve conflict, you have to work strategically in order to achieve unity. Remember, leaders take people not where they want to go, but where they *need* to go.

One negative emotion that can dismantle a team faster than a physical injury to a star player is envy. You *have* to avoid envy. It's a trap that will only hold you and your team back. It seems to me that people become envious of another person because that individual does something better than they do. Instead of being envious, the healthy thing to do is figure out how that person performs so well, because you will want him or her to be part of your team. This is a terrific time to ask the question, "How did you do that?"

When Michael Jordan was playing for the Chicago Bulls, and they were winning all of their championships, and he was considered by virtually everyone to be the best basketball player in the world, he created what he called the "Breakfast Club." On his own, Michael had been getting up early in the morning to train before practices, and was eating right to stay healthy. But he knew he couldn't win by himself, so he started to invite several of his teammates to join him in his "Breakfast Club." At club meetings, he shared the secrets of his success—for the good of the team.

Do you know that a lion trainer uses a stool to poke at the lion to confuse it? The legs on the stool perplex the lion and keep it from going into attack mode. I think people occasionally take this same approach: They jab stools at us to confuse us even more when we aren't sure what to do. We don't know which leg of the stool to attack, causing us lose our focus. My point is, there will always be weak-minded people who try to tear others down, to distract them from their focus on the greater goal. Great leaders overcome these distractions, in part by looking for integrity in the people they hire. Someone who lacks integrity will attempt to pull you down to his or her level to prevent you from being successful. Such people will cause confusion and divisiveness wherever they go. There's enough confusion in the workplace caused by external sources alone, so don't allow insiders to disrupt your team.

Are You Prepared?

Many elements of success lie in our own hands. First and foremost, you can prepare yourself to achieve what you want each and every day. Are you organized? Are your goals clear? Are your communications with others straightforward?

Keeping communication simple on game day will give you a *huge* advantage. I recall times when I walked out of huddles without having the first clue as to what the coach wanted because his or her direction was so disjointed. When I was in college, we routinely played to loud, sellout crowds, sometimes making it difficult to hear the plays that my coach was calling from the bench. In such times of poor communication, I used my natural leadership skills to make decisions for myself and the four other players on the floor with me. My coaches trusted and respected my attention to detail and preparation in those situations.

If you're leading people in business or sports, you must be able to communicate in a way that both they and you understand. Avoid talking down to people; instead, talk *with* them. Discuss. If you find yourself on the other side of criticism, accept it graciously. Don't fight everyone on every issue. Listen to your people. Consider their input. It might be worth giving their ideas a shot. Considering the ideas of others is another excellent way to build loyalty, trust, and respect among everybody on the team.

Do What It Takes

I can't tell you how many times I've walked into business meetings unsure of the outcome of the deal at hand. In the early 1990s, my company, Events Marketing, was launching a tennis event in Knoxville, Tennessee, for which we needed a title sponsor. I was sitting in the office of someone who was looking at my proposal; when he finished, he told me he didn't know if he could commit because it was a lot of money for a small market. I asked, "You play darts, Chris?" (I had noticed he had a dartboard on the back of his door and darts in a basket on his desk.) "Yes," he said, "I do play darts." Now that I had opened this door, I walked through it. "I'll throw you darts for the sponsorship," I said, only half in jest. "If you beat me, I'll leave. If I beat you, you're my title sponsor." Within minutes, there we were, throwing darts for the deal. I was thrilled when I won, because I knew how important this was for my company and the success of the event.

Of course I'm not saying that every business deal will be that easy, or that every interaction can be reduced to a game. And I'm sure you won't find this deal-making strategy in the books at Harvard Business School. What I am saying is that you *have* to be aware of your surroundings. Take a close look around at your environment. If you notice someone has Yankee memorabilia all over the room, use that information as a tool to bond. Tell a Yankee story— maybe about how you fell in love with Bucky Dent in 1978 when he hit a home run in a tiebreaker against the Red Sox. Do something, say something, that separates you from the rest.

To deal effectively with people you have to know how and when to pull out the stops. An important part of good communications is empathizing and being a good listener. Because women are such good multitaskers, we often take the initiative to ask the questions. But we also need to take the time to listen, really listen, to the answers, and observe. You must be able to read people. *How* you talk is as important as what you say. This is a skill you have to practice daily. Every day offers a brand-new opportunity to communicate properly with people in order to convince them to do what you want them to do!

To me, game time means that you're ready for the moment. You've put in your time and effort, and you've trained for this moment. You're prepared. You've done your homework. You understand your personnel. You know your market. You've made sacrifices to ensure that you and your team are ready. At game time, everything you've done, from chapter one through chapter nine, comes together. Game time is when the magic happens. We all come across a lot of people who can talk the game, about how great they are, the successes they've had. But when it's game time, it's time to put up or shut up.

I love the game of life and business because both are about delivering the goods. Did you execute the action? Did you make a change when it was appropriate? Do you have the confidence to lead people and to put it all on the line, time and again? Some people get antsy when they're practicing, because they care only about the game, whereas others excel in practice but lack confidence on game day. At some point, though, everyone has to play. That's why we run scrimmages and play exhibition games in sports: to learn to put everything on the line, look at ourselves, and make our corrections then, *before* game day.

When game day arrives, you have to be flexible and feel out the situation, because it's not always going to happen the way the experts say it will, or according to the playbook. For that reason, you have to be able to read people, assess the situation in the moment, and communicate—which, don't forget, includes being a good listener. In sports, we tell our players to play as hard as they can until the whistle. In basketball, we instruct players *not* to play for the time on the clock, but to play hard to the end, and to be prepared for the moments and opportunities that come only in the clutch. That's what makes the Warren Buffetts, Bill Gates, and Larry Ellisons of the world so special. You can be, too, if you arrive at game time with your skills fined honed and are willing to put everything you have on the line, to win.

Believe in Yourself

A big part of convincing people to follow your lead relates to how you handle yourself. You have to believe in yourself first. After all, you can't expect other people to trust you if you don't trust yourself. Embrace who you are. If you're confident about you, then you will be able to empower others.

I know this happens a lot: There's an office diva who walks around with an air about her, implying that she's better than everyone else. She's in charge, and you'd better be aware of it. If by chance, *you're* that person, then my advice is to drop the attitude—and fast. Acting like a prima donna is the quickest way to lose support and alienate yourself from those you're going to need down the road. Be real and make others feel good. Remember: It's not just about you.

I know women who want to work only for men because they've had such bad experiences working for women. As I discussed in an earlier chapter, females can be really tough on one another in the workplace. We talk about overcoming biases, but I find that, sometimes, the worst biases we face are from each other! It's unfortunate that there are circumstances in which we hold each other back. We can't always blame it on the guys. Sure, they frequently hold the keys to our success. And, sure, probably we're going to have to compete against other women for that "token spot" on the team; but we have to learn how to support each other, even when competing. Men are so good of taking care of each other in this way, and I applaud them for that. They hire and rehire each other time and time again. It reminds me of my days in the schoolyards watching the guys choosing their friends to play in pickup games. If you are already doing this, I raise my glass to you. Well done!

Here's a prime example. I was curious as to how Brian Winters got the job as the head coach of the WNBA Indiana Fever. I have known him since I was a teenager—not well, but enough to know he was a terrific shooter. One day, I found myself wondering, "How *did* he get one of the 13 most coveted jobs in women's basketball?"

As it turns out, when Brian was an All-American at South Carolina, a man named Donnie Walsh, now president of the New York Knicks, was one of South Carolina's assistant coaches. Brian was one of Donnie's first college recruits. Years later, when Donnie was CEO and president of the Indiana Pacers, he brought in his guy—Brian— whom he trusted—to coach and build his team.

Why don't women do things like this as a matter of practice? More often than not, they do the opposite, because they are afraid to have other women around. Some of this attitude stems from envy, or being concerned about putting another woman in a position where she might shine brighter than you, and maybe even take your spot. It also stems in part from sheer insecurity. I, for one, would much rather be around people who are smarter than I am. As I said before, if I'm the smartest one in the room, then we're in trouble. I love being around brilliant innovators and think-tank types, because I want to learn what they know.

Women need to work hard to leverage their positions and give others opportunities. I say, hire that young woman with all that energy, who's going to put forth an amazing amount of effort. She may not be experienced, but young people can be sweet, interesting, inquisitive, and fun. Most importantly, they're not jaded yet. Young people will keep *you* young; I adore having them around for their spunk, innocence, and fresh ideas. Blend that with experience and wisdom, and you have the ingredients for a solid, winning team.

Set Minigoals

I am a huge supporter of goal-setting. My whole life has been a series of minigoals—setting them and meeting them. First, I wanted to be the best player in my neighborhood. Next I wanted to test my skills at Rucker Park in Harlem against the guys. Then I wanted to make the U.S. Olympic team, then play in college, and then play professionally. I always have goals, as well as a plan for reaching them. I am a very visual person, as I said before, so I like to write things down. I love making lists, and I take great satisfaction in crossing things off of them.

I have a friend who works for Medtronic, one of the leading sales producers of defibrillators. Like me, she has always had a game plan, in her case, to work in sales for a Fortune 500 company. She began as a top earner in Medtronic's sales department, and has now been promoted into management. When she first started at the company, she would call me and say, "Oh my gosh. It is *so cool*. I was running my management meeting, and my people were listening to me . . . " Every time she called, she was very excited, because she was still learning. Everything was thrilling and new for her, and it was refreshing to sense her animation and hear her enthusiasm for her new position.

When you're a veteran and have experienced all of this previously, be sure not to put a damper on a newbie's enthusiasm. It might not be new to you, but it is to him or her. Likewise, resist the temptation to tell a rookie the horror stories of your own experience. *Don't.* Let them enjoy this time of growth, new experiences, and innocence. I am genuinely happy for my friend; she deserves this! So I build her up.

Having new energy on the team can be a refreshing experience for the veteran professional, as well. Many will remember Magic Johnson's first year in the NBA, 1979, when he was a rookie with the Lakers. The sports world became mesmerized by his smile, enthusiasm, and the effect he had not only on the fans but also on his own teammates. The media talked about the power of his smile to light up the arena. Magic's spirited nature was infectious for all of the Lakers. Even veteran all-star Kareem Abdul-Jabbar—who was then near the end of his career and always wore a stoic look on his face that seemed to warn, "Don't bother me, just let me be great"—was rejuvenated by Magic's presence on the team. I don't know who was more taken by the number of high-fives and chest bumps than Kareem himself that first season he played with Magic. I'm sure Kareem smiles now when he looks back at the Lakers' first game that season, when Magic jumped into his arms after winning a close one at the buzzer.

The message here: Stay positive and happy. I *guarantee* you will create more powerful alliances with that kind of attitude. If you're bringing an upbeat outlook into the workplace, instead of thriving on conflict, then you're on the right track. We must revel in each other's successes and assume that others will give you their best. Let's help each other get there.

Every woman who succeeds lays the groundwork for those coming after her. I take pride in knowing I'm setting the stage for another woman to be an NBA coach one day. Be someone who gives hope to others. Remember: *agree, disagree, and align.* This rule applies to women in general—to everyone, really. We must commit to being unified as we move forward, knowing that there will be ramifications today, tomorrow, and beyond. Let's produce and reinforce positive results, then set the bar even higher so other women have to work hard to achieve or surpass what we have already attained.

"B" Nice

We women endure different kinds of reactions and labeling than men do. I mean, wearing stilettos all day would make *anyone* angry, right? But, seriously, when we're assertive, we're often labeled with the B-word. (I prefer to think of it as "B" nice, though, as we all know, most others mean "bitch.") In contrast, when a man is assertive, he's labeled as "decisive"; he's said to be "on the fast-track to success"; he's admired for thinking that the "sky's the limit." Women, unfortunately, must maintain a delicate balancing act when they need to be assertive and proactive and delegate work. We have to accept this injustice even as we work to change the perception so that we can help other women who are trying to rise up through the ranks.

You can be nice, lighthearted, humorous, *and* strong and still be a woman who can run with the big dogs. Women get their feelings hurt and break into tears; men get their feelings hurt and act out. Even when guys aren't that secure, they still will try to convince others that they're strong, because they've been encouraged to behave that way since they were young. We need to take a cue from them, and learn to hold our ground even in adverse times.

Guys spend a lot of time teasing one another or being smart alecks, and this type of banter usually just rolls off their backs. Women, on the other hand, tend to communicate differently— again, we get our feelings hurt. When we do, we give away our power. Look at the influence of someone like Muhammad Ali. Long before the rap stars of today were doing it, he was using rhyming and rapping to draw people in, attract the spotlight, market his sport, and sell tickets. Men talk in sound bites. But women? We tell entire stories, which are frequently just *too long*. Men use periods on their statements, whereas women seem to prefer run-on sentences.

Women also tend to be compulsive confessors. A friend of mine who's a trial attorney coaches witnesses to *just answer the question*. Did you see the knife in his hand? Instead of simply replying, "No," a typical female answer might be, "No, but I knew there was one in the kitchen in the dishwasher. We used it last night." We like to hear ourselves talk when we should become more succinct wordsmiths. If we were paying by the word, many women would be bankrupt in no time. Try to approach conversation in a different way; be economic with your words—like we have to do when texting or tweeting. Simplify, shorten!

The way you say things impacts what people remember, so choose your words wisely. You want people to hear and value what you're saying. Here's a tip: When telling a story, be sure it has a point. It always makes it more enjoyable for the listener. (Oh, was that sarcastic?)

Take a Sound Bite Lesson

If you're in doubt about what you need to say, rehearse. I read out loud in front of a mirror. This is a great way to figure out how to edit your message, because you hear things when you speak aloud that you don't catch when you read silently. People laugh at me sometimes when I'm in a stadium before an event, because until the camera goes live, I continue to rehearse out loud—"The Celtics are two and a half games ahead of Orlando in the East. Kevin Garnett should be back tonight, and that should help the chemistry of the Boston Celtics." In television, we rehearse between every segment. We are given sheets that tell us how much time we have— Nancy: 40 seconds. Nancy: 20 seconds. I have to be concise, informative; give you an opinion and then back it up with "meat" (otherwise known as the facts) and deliver it all in 40 seconds, *without* sounding rushed.

Isn't this exactly what we're called upon to do in business when it's game time? We have to be prepared, consider our options, and rehearse what we're planning to tell our clients or team. We have to be concise and stay close to the core of what we're delivering. We're allowed to share an opinion, of course, but we have to back it up with facts. Give the necessary information to your listeners in the clearest way possible. Good business leaders are effective and *concise* communicators.

I use what I call my "two-minute" drill. Assume you're at a party, VIP reception, cocktail hour, or any event attended by people you need to get to know or meet, to network. With so much going on and so many people around, you really have only about two minutes to tell someone who you are, what you are there for, and what you need from them. Thus, two or three statements *have* to tell your whole story. If you get long-winded, you will in most cases lose the person's attention, and along with it your moment of opportunity. Another important tool in this type of situation is to never forget your business cards. Be prepared!

Observe People

In the movie *Erin Brockovich*, the title character, played by Julia Roberts, was chastised for wearing inappropriate clothing in the workplace. Though Erin took an "I-wear-what-I-like" stance on this matter, most employees would be humbled, and perhaps a bit embarrassed, by being confronted in this manner. If someone with whom you work is wearing clothing that just doesn't fly in the office, find an appropriate time and place to let her know that, for example, her skirt is too short or her blouse is too revealing. Handle this type of interaction with kindness and tact.

This is a skill we have to learn in sports, as well. Players are given warnings, or even technical fouls and penalties, if their jerseys are hanging out or their uniforms look sloppy. A dress code, how we're supposed to look on game day, is part of the emphasis that athletics places on professionalism. It's no different in a corporate office environment.

Same rule applies with tardiness. If someone is constantly late, you don't have to call them out in front of everybody. Find a time to bring it to his or her attention privately, and ask if there's any way you can help him or her to be on time.

If you're in a management position and it's your job to assess employees' performances, you have a lot of tools at your disposal: the budget, worksheet, marketing plan, PowerPoint presentation, or sales reports. It's a lot like using the stat sheet, film, or scouting reports to help you assess your team's performance in sports.

Game Time Rituals

Sports teams and individual players are notorious for engaging in game-time rituals. There's a lot of superstition in the world of sports. For example, we weren't permitted to wear jewelry during games when I was in college, so I would take the small medal I won in high school and tape it inside my high-top socks. And I always put on my left shoe first and my right shoe second. Many businesspeople are superstitious, too.

For instance, I have a friend who owns a multimillion-dollar car dealership in Dallas, Texas. One night we were getting ready to have dinner—his wife, brother-in-law, and me. He had just closed on a piece of property in Frisco, Texas, so we met him at the airport and then headed to Frisco before dinner. But we began heading in the wrong direction, so I asked where we were going. My friend's wife explained that he had just closed on some property and that he had a ritual every time this happened. We drove to this piece of property, where the two men got out of the car and peed on it. For luck. I was like, "You have *got* to be kidding me!" I asked, "How much is that piece of property worth?" When I found out, I wanted to go pee on it, too—if it was guaranteed to bring me the same amount of luck!

Everything about rituals and superstitions is mental. That medal I wore inside my sock in all of those games didn't *really* make me any better, but I *believed* it did. So it did. If you think you can win, you will. If you think you can't, it's almost certain that you won't. Game day rituals are important psychological motivators on game day. It works very much the same in business. If you think you're going to lose the deal, you probably will. If you believe you can win the deal, you have a much better chance of closing it. Use your mentality and mind-set to your advantage. Don't start out thinking, "Guys, we can't beat them, but we're going to keep it close." Keep *what* close? Why not try to be the best all the time?

You have to have faith in your good-luck charms if you're going to achieve the mind-set of a champion. *You* are your own good luck charm. It's that attitude that will exude a winning approach. And that's *not* superstition. You have done all the things necessary to set yourself up to be successful.

The great football coach Vince Lombardi is famous for saying, "Plan your work and work your plan." He's oft-quoted because it's so true. You have your team gathered in the locker room. You communicate the strategy of how you're going to win. You show your team how to be strategic thinkers. For good reason business-people are always quoting strategic gurus or sports clichés, some of which you've read throughout this book. But to make that kind of talk effective, you have to believe it. Winning comes down to three key elements: strategy, planning, and execution. That's the entire game, right there.

Risk/Reward

There's a fine line between recklessness and brilliance on game day. In Super Bowl XLIV, New Orleans Saints head coach Sean Payton was praised for instructing one of his players to make a "gutsy onside kick" to start the second half—a play that paid off big. When, 30 minutes later, Payton made another brazen decision, this time to go for a goal line, fourth down, he was referred to as a genius. He was taking *huge* risks and was being applauded because *they worked!* If they had failed, he would have been berated. What he did goes against traditional thinking. But the Saints won the Super Bowl, and life was good. If he had messed up, he would have heard remarks like, "What the *hell* was he thinking?"

The lesson here is to remember to enjoy the big wins, but reserve a little humility at the same time. At a luncheon I attended, I heard a fellow businesswoman repeat sage advice her father had once given her. He said that when you get a pat on the back, you have to remember that you're just six inches from getting a kick in the ass. Maintain some modesty when you're getting that pat on the back, and never forget that what goes up usually does come down. That's a good thing to keep in mind when you're at the top. A little humility will soften the fall, if or when it comes.

It's Okay to Be Great

There's nothing wrong with being audacious. The Connecticut women's basketball team has one of the longest winning streaks in history—78 games recorded for the first time ever in back-to-back undefeated seasons with NCAA Division I Championship titles in 2009 and 2010. People have asked me if this kind of winning streak is somehow "wrong." I retort, was it wrong for Nike to want to crush Adidas? For Apple to want to win over PCs? You can't hold back if you really want to win. You can't "play nice." You have to play freely, and energize those around you.

Greatness is a pursuit, one that starts within you. When I first started training Martina Navratilova in the early 1980s, I asked her what her goals were. She said she wanted to be the greatest shot maker of all time. And I said, *really?* Why? She replied that she wanted to hit shots that no one else could. Again, I said, *really?* Then I extended the question: You would rather make the "wow" shots during a match than be a consistent winner? Do you want the "wow" factor, or the *win* factor?

Don't go for the wow factor on game day; instead, vie for success. I have never wanted to be what I call a "Dow Jones-er," going up, down, up, down. I want to be consistently consistent in my life. I have always viewed skeptically the people who say, "I've won millions and lost millions." Those people scare me to death. You *always* want to "be in the money" in your career. Every business book that Harvey Mackay writes is a top seller—notably, *Swim with the Sharks (without Being Eaten Alive)*, *Beware the Naked Man Who Offers You His Shirt*, and *Dig Your Well before You're Thirsty*—because he puts forth consistent theories and information. You want that kind of steadiness in your professional life. If you develop a certain level of expectation, prepare yourself, and expect success, you will get it.

We all think we're aficionados and experts and great "guys," but those are adjectives we throw at people. They told us at ESPN to stop with the adjectives. Too often after we said, "He's such a great guy," the next day that great guy had been arrested on a DUI. We're a society unafraid to blurt things out then hope they hold credence. I always say, *you can't control your reputation, but you can control your character*. I'm not always in charge of the outcome on game day, but I am in control of how hard I choose to prepare and play.

Decision Makers

As a leader you have tremendous responsibility. Los Angeles Clippers head Coach Vinny Del Negro told me this: "I listen to everything my assistant coaches tell me. I hear all of their suggestions, but then *I* make the decision. Until you're in my seat, you can't know the responsibility of making the choice that determines whether you win or lose."

At one point several years ago, Tiger Woods was planning to leave IMG and his agent Hughes Norton. My agent at the time—IMG's Mark Steinberg—was told to drop all of his clients to focus solely on Tiger. Though it meant breaking off other ties at the time, Mark and Tiger joined forces and found that they were the right match—both in business and on a personal level. Mark has become one of Tiger's dearest friends and most trusted advisors.

If you're going to play the game of life, play to the best of your ability. Somebody's going to get the job, why not you? Somebody's going to get the scholarship, why not you? Put yourself in a position for it to *be* you: do the work and have the right attitude.

This playbook is a compilation of the strategies, mental preparation, and execution and belief systems that you need to implement so that you can do whatever it is you want to do, and play to win. I know I repeat myself often, but to excel at something, you must do it repetitively—over and over and over again. (See?)

As Warren Buffett learned so long ago from his high school basketball coach: Don't take the shot unless you know you're going to make it. Don't make a deal just for the sake of making a deal; do something that can make you a winner. Don't just show up. My mother can *technically* shoot a basketball, but can she make it? Probably not. Anyone can show up at work and hand in a piece of paper, but is there anything of quality on it? If you're going to do something, be the best at it.

Every woman needs a *Playbook for Success* to know where she's starting, where she's going, and how to get there. But remember, it's not worth the effort if life isn't fun along the way. There are so many things that can sully your day. Maintaining your sense of humor, engaging in friendly banter and rivalries, meeting challenges, and being able to go to the wall with people you like and have mentored—or have mentored you—are what make life and work enjoyable. Tap into the power of belief and be willing to incorporate change and constantly push the limits of who you are. That's what makes it all worthwhile.

Is It in You?

One day, sitting in the living room at my home in Detroit, where I was then coaching, I was watching ESPN *Sports Center* with my husband at the time, Tim, and our son, TJ, who was three. The anchor, Dan Patrick, said, "Today's a sad day in sports because the greatest basketball player in history, Michael Jordan, is retiring." TJ leaned over, looked at me, and said, "Mommy, you told me you were the greatest basketball player of all time." I stammered around a bit before I replied, "Uh, well, they don't want Michael to feel bad, so they're telling the story this way about him on *Sports Center*." Tim looked at me and said, "What do you tell this kid when I'm not around?"

I told TJ the truth—*my* truth. The truth is that you, too, can be the greatest of all time. You just have to want to be!

Sports Talk—Glossary

A

Always on the ball   Reliable, on top of it, knowing what needs to be done.

B

Ball is in your court   You have to make the decision.

Bases are loaded   A good chance, or potential for success.

Basketball ready   Being alert, because anything can happen at any moment.

Bottom of the ninth   The final stages; time to make something happen; the end is in sight.

C

Call another play   Change the strategy.

Call the shots   Makes the decisions.

Carry the ball   Be in control.

Coaching people up   Coaching people to another level.

Curveball   An unexpected event or action; keeps others off balance.

D

Double-team   Put the pressure on someone/several people.

Down the home stretch   Almost there; goal is in sight; last phase.

F

Foul   Unfair, against the rules.

Fumble   A setback.

G

Game plan   Strategy.

Get off the blocks   Have a good start.

Get to first base   Make the first step, but no guarantee of going farther.

H

He went yard   He reached his goal.

Hit a home run   Achieved the ultimate goal.

Hitter   Person who performs well.

Hole-in-one   Success on the first try.

Homerun hitter   Person who performs exceptionally well.

Huddle up   Have a group meeting.

I

I was in the zone   Everything was working for me.

It's a layup   It's simple.

It's in your wheelhouse   You can make this happen.

It's the fourth quarter   Time is running out, and the end is in sight.

M

Man down   When the other team is "man down," your team has the
advantage.

Middle of the fairway   In a great position.

My dog   He/she is loyal to me.

O

On deck circle   You're up next, be ready; you're almost on the inside.

Out of the park   Reached your ultimate goal.

P

Pinch hitter   A person who comes in to take someone else's place; a troubleshooter.

Play hardball   Be aggressive.

Power play   Have the advantage.

Put the press on them   Apply pressure.

Q

Quarterback   The individual who runs the show, makes the calls; the "brain" or most important person.

R

Rainout   Future benefit.

Red zone   The area in which to achieve your goal; very close to "making it."

Rookie move   An attempt by an inexperienced person.

Run with it   Go with an idea; try it out.

S

Scouting report   Information on your competition.

Send him down to the minors   Demote someone.

Shutout   Failure to accomplish objective or reach goal.

Slam dunk   Certainty; a foregone conclusion.

Starting gate   Beginning.

Sudden death   Now or never.

T

Team player   A person who wants the best for the team; unselfish.

Tee it up   Set up to succeed.

Three strikes   Failure to reach goal; setback; interruption.

Turnover   Loss of an opportunity; giving the other side a chance.

Two-minute warning   Need to make something happen—now.

Two-point conversion   Take a chance for greater advantage.

V

Veteran   Experienced professional.

W

We're on the clock   Time to make a decision.

Y

You're going to run the point   You're taking the lead.

INDEX